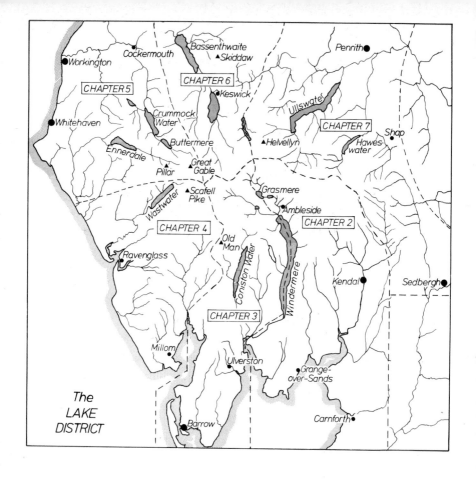

The
LAKE
DISTRICT

A Visitor's Guide To
—THE—
LAKE DISTRICT

Brian Spencer

Moorland Publishing

ISBN 0 86190 010 3 (paperback)
0 86190 013 8 (hardback)

Typeset by Alacrity Phototypesetters,
Banwell Castle, Weston-super-Mare, Avon
and printed in Great Britain by
Redwood Burn Ltd, Trowbridge & Esher
for Moorland Publishing Co Ltd,
PO Box 2, Ashbourne, Derbyshire DE6 1DZ

Contents

Illustrations

Shap Abbey / 120
Thunder Stone / 122

Sources of illustrations: British Tourist Authority p30, 44-5, 48, 56-7, 80-1, 84-5, 87, 100-1, 103, 106-7; Geoffrey Berry p35. All remaining photographs were taken by the author.

Panoramic Views from:

The panoramic views are based on those originally published in *Black's Picturesque Guide to the English Lakes* (1858) with the addition of current place-names, but these give a very convenient way of identifying the mountains and fells of Lakeland.

Preface

Note on the Walks Described

The walks suggested in this book are not intended to be a field-by-field guide, but recommendations for the best routes. Many have been chosen so that they avoid the popular and crowded areas, while many are more interesting or give better views than the better known routes. Walkers must be equipped according to the severity of the terrain: a lakeside stroll or woodland walk requires only stout shoes and weather protection. High level mountain walks need proper boots and clothing, map and compass and the ability to use them correctly. The Ordnance Survey 1:25,000 *Outdoor Leisure Map of the English Lakes* in four sheets is strongly recommended.

Up-to-date local weather reports can be obtained by telephoning Windermere 5151.

Mountain Rescue: telephone 999 and ask for mountain rescue.

The walks described have been graded so that a suitable route may be chosen at a glance. Both distance and walking time are included, but the latter is often of more relevance.

H	High level route for fine weather conditions
M	Medium level route
L	Low level route, often recommended when the weather in the mountains is poor
*	Well signposted
**	Easy to follow with the aid of a map
***	Requires careful map reading
****	Recommended for experienced hill walkers only
o	Least interest
oo	
ooo	
oooo	Most interest

1 The English Lake District

Why the *Lake* District? The question is often asked in all seriousness, for after all the area does have the finest and highest mountains in England. It is these mountains which create the setting for the lakes and tarns and provide the backcloth to the beauty that is the English Lake District. Although small in area when compared with the Alps or even the Highlands of Scotland, being little more than 880 square miles in area, it is the mecca for thousands who annually seek out its delights. It is an area of unique beauty with the spectacular grandure of its mountains and the sylvan-beauty of its lakes set in lovely dales, that has easy access from the rest of the country since the M6 motorway was built.

How can the visitor see this area best? The very best view of all is from an early morning flight from Manchester to Glasgow. The short haul route is usually via Coniston Lake and then to the east of England's highest point — Scafell Pike. If you take this flight in early spring when the ridges are still etched with snow and if you are lucky to have a clear day the whole glory of the lakes, tarns and fells reveal themselves in a tantalising living map. As the jet goes over the summit of Skiddaw there will be few who cannot resist a backward glance as the suns rays touch the high tops.

The story of how these mountains and lakes came to be is long and ever changing. The fells we see today are the remains of a huge mountain dome created by raising the remains of even older rocks originally deposited in an ancient tropical sea which existed about 400 million years ago. As the grand design which created the modern hills started, pressures from land masses to the north

pushed so that the dome gradually rose then cracked. These cracks became valleys which in time were deepened by the action of glaciers from the ice ages of the most recent past, in geological terms. Running water altered the landscape and continues to this day to help the erosion of wind and frost to wear down even the mightiest summit. Natural, and later man-made, damming created the lakes and tarns of the higher regions.

Man has lived on the lakeland fells for at least five thousand years, and probably first came here to hunt in the forests which once densely covered the whole district. Most of the fells we know today would once have been covered by trees which gradually died back with changes in weather patterns and clearance as later men became settlers and farmed the lower slopes.

Industry came early to the Lakes. The green volcanic rocks outcropping around the head of Great Langdale were recognised very early on in the Stone Age. Seasonal 'factories' were set up to work the screes such as the one below Pike of Stickle and many rejects or partly finished stone axes have been found. It is easy to imagine the ringing sound of stone against stone as these early people roughed out their axes and spear heads high up on the valley sides. The final polishing was carried out closer to the sea around Ravenglass, before the finished products were exported around the coasts of the British Isles and even further afield to Ireland and Britanny.

With the civilising effect of farm husbandry the need for calendars to regulate time brought about the building of stone circles such as the spectacular one of Castlerigg near Keswick. Gradually tribes formed and with the tactical advantage of steep mountains and remote hidden valleys to help them they must have made life pretty difficult indeed for the Roman legions who eventually came this way. Remains of several Roman forts are here but nowhere is there any indication of anything other than a military occupation. The Romans built their roads as high as possible to keep out of danger and one can only guess at the misery of a legionary marching along the track which follows the long ridge of High Street on its way to the garrison town that became modern Carlisle away on Rome's north-west frontier.

The Romans did not come up here just to keep the tribes in order, but more likely they would be interested in the metals found beneath the ground. Mining for a wide variety of minerals, especially copper and lead, was a major industry until recent times.

The Viking settlers left their mark in many of the place names we know today; names like Greta (griot à, the rocky or gravelly river), Ullswater (Ulif's lake), Birkrigg (Birch ridge), are a few examples. Later settlers came of Irish-Scandinavian stock and left place names such as Birker (birch tree shieling); Patterdale (Pattraicc's valley).

During the period of Norman domination the land was mostly divided up amongst the abbeys of Furness, Holm Cultram and St Bees. Until the formation of the abbeys dense forest covered much of the country around and even the highest fells have had some covering of dwarf scrubby birch. The monks developed a woollen industry by opening up large areas of moorland as sheep walks and so, unwittingly, set the scene which we see today. Birds of prey such as the eagle soon disappeared and the wild boar, a creature of the forest, went by the thirteenth century. The wolf was once common, but was not allowed to exist in sheep country. Boars and wolves have

never made a comeback, but the large birds of prey are now occasionally to be found in remote coombes and valley heads.

The many miles of dry-stone walls built in the period between 1750 and 1850 stand even now as a memorial to other men's work on the land. However, it is modern twentieth-century man who has carried out the most drastic alterations to the face of the Lake District with forestry developments, deepening existing lakes, and in some cases creating new lakes. Some of these developments have been an improvement on nature, but some of the regimented forest schemes leave much to be desired.

During the romantic era of the late eighteenth and early nineteenth centuries poets and artists discovered the Lakes. They were the forerunners of the tourists who have increased from the handful — once so small that Dorothy Wordsworth was able to record the numbers who passed Dove Cottage at Grasmere — to the thousands who go there today for recreation and enjoyment. William Wordsworth was probably the first fell-walker to travel the hills purely for the love of their grandure and the solitude they offered.

Property ownership has seen a dramatic change in the past decade or so. The mansions of northern industrialists adorning prime vantage spots along the lake shores are now likely to be hotels or outdoor pursuit centres, while the quarryman's cottage in Borrowdale will probably now be someone's holiday home. The demand for such accommodation, if unchecked, could have produced hideous caravan camps almost everywhere. Growing popularity of the Lakes as a holiday and amenity area made some sort of control necessary to cater for tastes as widely diverse as power boat racing to bird watching. The Lake District is so small and vulnerable that it would be easy to spoil it for ever. With far sightedness many landowners willed land and property to the National Trust in safe keeping for future generations. In 1951 the Lake District National Park Board was formed to carry out the necessary function of controlling land use and development of all kinds. As well as control the board provide useful services as diverse as organising guided walks to help newcomers and regular visitors alike, as well as audio-visual displays and lectures on Lake District topics, based on their Brockhole Visitor Centre.

Moving to the present time we have more leisure than ever before, and more and more people have discovered the challenge and beauty of the mountains and lakes, with the result that the more popular areas rapidly become overcrowded. Traffic control plans to ban cars from the more crowded areas are as yet controversial, but the time cannot be far away when whole areas will be free of all but local or essential traffic. It has been proved to work in other parts of the country, such as in the Goyt Valley in the Peak District. With such a traffic control system tourists leave their cars at strategically placed car parks outside the district and then use the frequent buses to ride into the area of their choice. One of the main advantages of this scheme is that it encourages motorised tourists to become pedestrians, and so they are able to explore more of the countryside than perhaps they would if faced with the problem of driving along crowded narrow winding roads. The Lake District already has an excellent network of bus routes provided by such diverse organisations as the Post Office Post Bus Service and the Mountain Goat Bus Company, as well as the more traditional transport companies operating in the area. A miniature railway and lake steamers complete the system.

One of the main aims in writing this guide is to encourage the tourist to become more selective in his or her holiday travels. The Lake District is popular and deservedly so, but it is an area highly vulnerable to over use. However there is no need to feel that we will destroy it by coming here, for if everyone respects what they enjoy without leaving litter, and if they keep to proper footpaths and resist the temptation to take short cuts, which only lead to erosion, then this jewel will remain for the delight of future generations. After that, what is there for the tourst and holiday maker to do in the Lakes. Plenty! Gone are the days of cheap petrol so there is no advantage to be gained from motoring around without any firm plan in mind. The best idea is to take a section at a time, use the car or public transport as a means of access and then get out on foot to look at everything around. It is much more interesting to see the countryside close to, rather than view it through a car windscreen.

What do you want to do when you come to Lakeland? The main activities can be considered under the headings of water, walking, education, leisure and food. Water recreation is well catered for whether you are an angler, canoeist, if you sail, drive a power boat, or want to sit back and enjoy the nostalgia of a trip on one of the old steamers still very active on Windermere. Walkers can find enough for a lifetime's holidays before exhausting the possibilities, either high in the mountains or down in the valleys. Education is catered for at the many centres, both public and private. Leisure activities are organised by the National Park Centre at Brockhole, or you can visit one of the many famous country houses in and around the Lakes. You can also watch the locals enjoying themselves at the sporting events that are held at Grasmere. Marvel at the speed at which the runners dash up and down local fells. What you perhaps took several hours over, they are up and down in minutes! If you are of a sporting nature then go to one of the many hound trailing events and match your judgement against that of the locals. Hound trailing is very much a spectator sport, even though it is one where the object of everyone's attention is more out of sight than in. Food — well everyone has their favourite — either the simple tea room, the pub with its traditional fare or the cuisine of many of the high class restaurants and hotels round and about. A lot of fun can be had in finding your own ideal eating place, but the best ones are usually the least well advertised.

Not everyone is lucky enough to enjoy fine weather on their holiday. Mountains attract rain, or how else would all those lakes get filled? In particularly bad weather keep off the fells unless you really are an expert — there are plenty of lower level walks as we shall find out in later chapters. Often on rainy days in the more central areas you will find sunshine down on the coast at Grange or Furness or along the north shore of Morecambe Bay. Wet days can be well spent finding what the Brockhole and Grizedale Centres have to offer. There really is no excuse for wandering aimlessly around the shops and tourist traps of Keswick and Windermere.

How do you reach the Lake District? Like most you will probably come by road either from the north, east, or south. This means that eventually you will be using the M6 or A6 to get there and entering by the A66 Penrith to Keswick road or on to the A591 after bypassing Kendal. Or possibly if you want to get to the western lakes you would use the A590 Levens-Barrow road. These three roads take the brunt of visitor traffic to the Lake District, with good dual carriageway roads for part of their length, but even so they do get crowded at peak times. Although it is not easy, it is possible to avoid the bulk of holiday traffic by careful use of the Ordnance Survey map and journey along minor roads rather than the main thoroughfares. Who

knows, this way you might find that off-the-route pub or beautyspot that few others know about. It is possible but, as inferred earlier, it takes a little more trouble.

The Lake District can be divided into segments or regions almost indefinitely, each with its own characteristics varying at almost every turn. This book has divided the Lake District into six sections each having a chapter to itself. Each chapter will attempt to describe everything there is to see and do there. Hopefully it will encourage the reader to want to explore more of this charming and beautiful area known as the English Lake District. The activities range from visiting stately homes to fell walking. Each section differs widely from its neighbour, for instance, compare the Windermere area with Wastwater. In the former with its gentler terrain, more country estates are found and the description obviously dwells on them, but Wastwater is much wilder and more remote and the activities there will be more energetic. Some areas are quiet and remote and yet others can be very crowded at busy times.

Few, if any, of the properties (both privately owned and National Trust) are open seven days a week, so before deciding to visit any of them it is best to check either by a phone call, or better still to consult the latest edition of the Lake District National Park Information Sheet on the subject. Details of these and other sources of information are at the end of this book.

A varied selection of graded walks are described in each chapter. All should be within the capabilities of the average fit visitor, but however experienced you are, never go out without the basic equipment of adequate clothing and map and compass. Remember, it will be several degrees colder on top of the fells than it was in the valley bottom. Weather changes dramatically in mountainous country, especially in the English Lake District which has the added proximity to the Irish Sea to bring in sudden storms.

The descriptions of the walks assumes the walker will be using the new 1:25000 Ordnance Survey Maps of the English Lakes, which cover the region on four sheets. These new additions to the range of OS maps show a wealth of clear and easily followed detail; they are an invaluable aid to an enjoyable holiday. Descriptions of walks which dwell on a wealth of detail are often confusing and sometimes out of date due to the removal of walls, stiles, etc, so the walks described in this book give the main features such as farm names, fell summits or path junctions as these can be readily interpreted on the map. Take the bus or your car for a short distance and take your time exploring this delectable area, there cannot be anyone who can honestly say that they have found everything there is to be seen in the English Lake District.

2 Kendal to Grasmere

The most obvious route for the visitor travelling north to this south-eastern end of the Lake District will be along the M6 motorway and on to the Kendal bypass. Instead of continuing northwards there is an attractive introductory deviation into Kendal as this is now a more relaxed place since the volume of traffic in the town has become a mere fraction of what it was before the coming of the motorway. When the northern section of motorway was opened it was around midday; office and shop workers who had taken their lives into their hands crossing the A6 in the town centre on their way to lunch were suddenly confronted with an almost eerie emptiness on their return only minutes later. Heavy traffic had just disappeared.

Kendal is again a pleasant old town with its present formation dating from the bloody days of border warfare. The castle is a reminder of this period of history; it was built after a particularly terrible massacre of the people of Kentdale by Scots under Duncan, Earl of Fife.

Kendal High Street

Kendal Church and gateway

Katherine Parr the last of Henry VIII's wives was born here. Not as frequently married as Henry, nevertheless she managed four husbands (Henry was her third).

A more notable, but not readily recognised link with Border days is the way a number of old houses in the town are grouped around yards which are entered by narrow alleys. Careful scrutiny will often show traces of old doorways in the alleys which could be bolted and barred. In this way the citizens of Kendal slept safe in their beds at night.

A basket hilted sword hanging in Kendal church is said to be a link with the Civil War. Apparently it belonged to Robert Phillipson, a Cavalier known also as Robert the Devil, who lived at Belle Isle on Windermere. Robert had been besieged by Roundhead troops and when the siege was lifted he sought revenge on his enemies who he thought were at prayer in Kendal church. He interrupted the church service by riding with his troop of horsemen up the chancel, but fortunately the Parliamentary troops had moved on. An unlucky townsman who

Bridge over the River Kent, Kendal

tried to stop the intrusion was killed and Robert lost his sword in his hasty exit. Another military link inside the church is an Imperial Dragon Flag captured in the Chinese war. This hangs alongside the complete set of Westmorland Regiment's colours, dating back to its formation in 1755.

Charles Stuart the Young Pretender came through here and slept at No 95 Stricklandgate, which is now known locally as Prince Charlie's House. He spent two nights here, one on his way south in a vain attempt to claim the English Crown. His second stay was after his return from Derby, but this time he led a sorry band of stragglers who were being hotly pursued by the Hanoverian troops only two days behind.

Kendal is a busy town with industries as diverse as snuff making to shoe manufacturing. It is an excellent shop-ping centre, well worth lingering over especially now that the problem of heavy traffic has disappeared. Close by the church is the Abbot Hall Art Gallery and Museum of Lakeland Life and Industry. The latter deals with man's impact on the Lakeland landscape since prehistoric times as well as housing a fine collection of old farm and industrial tools and implements.

Just south of Kendal and by a bend in the River Kent at Watercrook stands the remains of the Roman fort of Alavna. It was built to defend the valley from invasion from the sea. Very little has been excavated, but coins and an altar found in 1930 are on view at Abbot Hall Museum.

There are plenty of things to see to the south of Kendal to make a delay worth while. Sizergh Castle has been home of the Strickland family for over seven hun-

PLACES TO VISIT NEAR KENDAL

Abbot Hall Art Gallery

Abbot Hall was built in 1759 by John Carr of York and houses the art gallery. The ground floor contains period furnished rooms with furniture, paintings, silver, china, glass. Paintings are by well-known artists such as George Romney, Sir Joshua Reynolds, J. M. W. Turner and John Ruskin. Upper floor has modern galleries with paintings, sculpture, prints, pottery, embroidery and other crafts.

Museum of Lakeland Life and Industry

Housed in the stable block of Abbot Hall and has period rooms displaying costumes, printing, weaving, children's toys, domestic and farming byegones, and local industries. In particular there is a farmhouse parlour furnished as it would have been last century, and a classroom from the Old Grammar School, Kendal.

Kendal Borough Museum, Station Rd
Displays of natural history, local history, early man, and domestic equipment. Roman, Egyptian and general interest. There is a large collection of birds (especially from Lakeland).

Castle Dairy, Wildman Street, Kendal
The house was originally the dairy for Kendal Castle. The oldest habitable stone-built house in the area, with many interesting period features including a carved four-poster bed.

Kendal Castle

Ruins of twelfth-century and later building in public park. The home of Katherine Parr.

The oldest part is a fourteenth-century pele tower or block house into which the locals would hide themselves and their animals in safety whenever the marauding Scots came around.

A couple of miles downstream is Levens Hall but even though its origins are even older than Sizergh this fine example of an Elizabethan Mansion has seen many owners in its life. The glory of Levens is in the fine collection of topiary or shaped yew trees which are rightly acknowledged as the best in the country. A curious tale is told in connection with the deer park across the road from Levens. Tradition has it that a traveller about 200 years ago who was denied refreshment by the staff of the hall put a curse on the place, the effect of which was that no male heir would be born to Levens Hall until the river Kent ran dry and a white stag born in the park. The curse ran true and was fulfilled in 1895 when the river Kent was frozen solid and a pale fawn stag appeared in the park. On the 20th February 1896 Alan Desmond Bagot was born. Another version of the tale is that a white stag predicts important events at Levens.

Still moving away from central Lakeland, but indicative of the wealth of interest in the countryside and towns surrounding its boundaries, lies what is probably the best vantage point to view the majesty of the range of Lakeland Fells. The peninsular south of the river Kent bounded by Milnthorpe, Beetham, the Yealands, Silverdale and Arnside is a sun trap often enjoying superb weather while the northern hills are shut in with rain clouds. Partly composed of limestone this little corner with miniature crags and small forests has flowers and trees to delight the eye of anyone prepared to stop and look around. At Beetham the Fairy Steps — a natural staircase in the limestone — is massed with ferns throughout the summer months.

dred years and is more than enough excuse to delay northward exploration. The ancient grey walls are set amongst bright flower beds and hold a unique collection of Stuart and Jacobean relics.

Sizergh Castle△

Topiary Gardens, Levens Hall ▽

Sizergh Castle (National Trust), 3 m south of Kendal near A6/A591 interchange

Fourteenth-fifteenth century castle including a 60 ft pele tower with some original fireplaces, floors and windows; Great Hall added in 1450 but altered and decorated in later centuries when the wings, with fine pannelling and interior decoration were added. Contains English and French furniture, silver, china, family portraits, Stuart and Jacobean relics.

Levens Hall, 5 m south of Kendal, on the A6

Norman pele tower converted to a magnificent Elizabethan mansion containing fine panelling, plasterwork, paintings and furniture; famous topiary garden laid out in 1692. Steam collection with working models of stationary steam and hot air engines; full scale showman's traction engine, steam wagon and steam car in steam on Sundays. Six-inch scale model gives rides.

Heron Corn Mills, Beetham, 1 m south of Milnthorpe

A rural water powered cornmill, built about 1730 on the foundations of an earlier mill and operating commercially until 1955, using four pairs of millstones. Restored to give regular demonstrations.

Leighton Hall, near Yealand

An eighteenth-century 'Gothick' Hall, the home of the Gillow family, famous as makers of high class furniture. The hall contains much early Gillow furniture, pictures and one of the world's largest dolls houses. Collection of birds of prey, with eagles flown free in afternoons, weather permitting.

Steamtown Railway Museum, Warton Road, Carnforth

Largest railway centre in the north west with a magnificent collection of preserved steam locomotives, including the *Flying Scotsman* and *Sir Nigel Gresley*. There are other locomotives from Britain, France and Germany, plus vintage coaches, signal box, model railway, 15 in gauge railway. Regular steam rides in the summer.

Flying Scotsman *at Steamtown, Carnforth*

Heron Corn Mills at Beetham offer demonstrations of corn grinding with original equipment in a rural watermill which is one of the largest of its type in the north. The mill is believed to have been built about 1730 on the foundation of an older mill which had been in existence since 1220 AD. The mill was still operating commercially up to 1955.

Leighton Hall at Silverdale only 1½ miles north of Junction 35 on the M6 is the home of the Gillow family and it houses a collection of furniture special to their name. Outside attractions centre on the collection of birds of prey with eagles which are flown every fine afternoon.

Steamtown Railway Museum at Carnforth is a must for steam enthusiasts coming this way. It houses a large collection of steam locomotives and frequently offers steam excursions throughout the north west.

Detail of Flying Scotsman, *Carnforth*

Morecambe Bay sands

A guide to the Lake District devoting so much space suggesting to the tourist that he looks around before venturing into the central areas must have something special to offer at this stage. As a novel approach to the mountains why not start by walking in from sea level? There have been routes across Morecambe Bay at low tide since Tudor times and maybe before. The main route runs across the sands from Bolton-le-Sands below Carnforth to Grange-over-Sands on the far side. In the days before roads had good surfaces the crossing saved something like fourteen miles; since Henry VIII's time a guide has been available to show the route as it varies from day-to-day through belts of quick-sand and deep channels of the Kent estuary. Guide's Farm a mile or so to the south west of Grange is still there and is the perquisite of the man who has the job of

L
10m
4½h
**
ooo

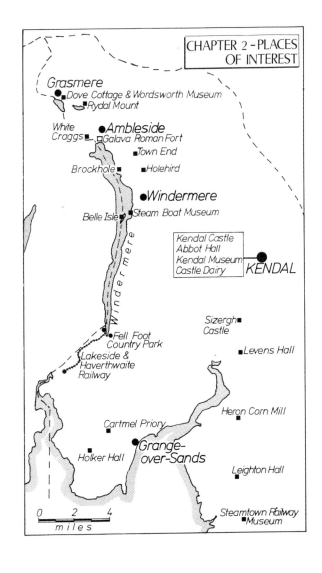

CHAPTER 2 – PLACES OF INTEREST

Grasmere
● Dove Cottage & Wordsworth Museum
■ Rydal Mount

White Craggs ■
● Ambleside
□ Galava Roman Fort
■ Town End

Brockhole ■   ■ Holehird

● Windermere

Belle Isle ▼ ■ Steam Boat Museum

Kendal Castle
Abbot Hall
Kendal Museum
Castle Dairy
● KENDAL

Windermere

Sizergh ■ Castle

● Fell Foot Country Park
Lakeside & Haverthwaite Railway

■ Levens Hall

Heron Corn Mill ■

Cartmel Priory ■
● Grange-over-Sands
■ Holker Hall

Leighton Hall ■

Steamtown Railway ■ Museum

0   2   4
miles

21

proving the route three times a week. Anyone who is interested in making the crossing should make enquiries through Mr C. Robinson, Guides Farm, Cart Lane, Grange-over-Sands. Telephone Grange-over-Sands 2165. Mr Robinson organises crossings with small parties depending on tides and weather throughout the summer months. **On no account should unaccompanied crossings be contemplated. The sands are dangerous and tides come in very fast.**

An interesting feature of the Morecambe Bay crossing which walkers making the ten mile treck will see is the ancient practice of fluke-fishing. This is a method of fishing where nets are stretched across upright poles driven into the sand at low tide. When the tide comes in fish swim into the nets and are gathered at the next low tide. Mussel and shrimp collecting is done from specially adapted high lorries which go out at low tide.

Grange-over-Sands is a natural suntrap and can justifiably claim the title of the 'Torquay of the North'.. It cannot claim to be the same size or offer the same amenities as its Devonshire counterpart, but the gentle climate of the place is clearly indicated by the profusion of flower gardens, both private and municipal. Certainly it is a superb setting for this quiet retreat between mountains and the sea.

In the quiet south-west corner between the Lakes and the sea is a maze of byways and low lying fells suitable for all-weather walks. Ancient villages have many links with the past. Villages like Cartmel with its Priory Church and gatehouse are now the only relic of past glory remaining after the dissolution of monasteries in the reign of Henry VIII. Legend says that the priory was built by Irish monks who on divine instructions searched for a valley with water flowing north and south. After months of searching they found what they were looking for almost at the very spot where they had earlier landed in Lakeland.

Holker Hall, about four miles to the west of Grange-over-Sands, is an occupied stately home open to the public. Set in 200 acres of deer park its attractions feature hot air ballooning and parascending on suitable days as well as a children's farm and an adventure playground. The gardens have many plants which are not normally found growing in the North of England and this is a sure indication of the mild climate of this little corner. A recently opened motor museum is a feature and special events are planned annually.

Having at last arrived in the Lake District there is still a large area of country bordering on Lake Windermere

---

PLACES TO VISIT NEAR GRANGE-OVER-SANDS:

Holker Hall, Cark-in-Cartmel, 4 m west of Grange-over-Sands
Home of the Cavendish family in a 22-acre garden set out by the seventh Duke of Devonshire, with rhododendrons and rare trees. Large park with herds of deer. Originally a sixteenth-century house, a new wing was built in 1872 after a fire and this contains interesting carvings, stonework, furniture and paintings. There is a motor museum, a countryside museum, curio and inventions museum, large-guage model railway, a play area, children's farm and an exhibition on running a large estate.

Cartmel Priory Gatehouse (National Trust), 5 m south of Newby Bridge
All that remains (apart from the church) of an Augustinian priory dating from about 1330. A picturesque building in Cartmel village, once used as a grammar school from 1624 to 1790, it is now a craft centre and shop.

which is often ignored and is yet well worth lingering over. North of Grange the fells above the village of Lindale can rightly be said to be the start of Lakeland. Lindale was the home of John Wilkinson the eighteenth-century iron master who was one of the leading figures of the Industrial Revolution.

Newton Fell to the west of the River Winster and Whitbarrow Scar to the east, do not have many official rights of way across their tops, but by careful map reading several pleasant routes can be worked out on east to west crossings. A gentle circular walk from Underbarrow a little to the north leads to the village of Crook by way of Capplerigg Lane; on to Crook Hall and Low Fold and back to Underbarrow. The walk is only about 3½ miles and an ideal way to limber up for more energetic outings later on.

L
3½m
2h
*
oo

There are two Staveleys in this area, the larger one is in the north in Westmorland and shelters at the bottom of the Kentdale Valley where it broadens out into the fertile plain of the river Kent. Lancashire's Staveley at the bottom end of Windermere is a quiet corner usually missed by the throngs rushing up to Lakeside to board Windermere steamers. This Staveley was the home of a William Robinson who died at the age of only twenty eight, but left several bequests to ensure his remembrance in later years. One of these which gives a link with the Morecambe Bay crossing was for the interest of £20 to be given annually to the 'Guide of Lancaster Sands'.

Nearby Newby Bridge has a pretty bridge spanning the River Leven which runs only a short distance from Windermere to its estuary below Greenodd. Although short in length, it is full of beauty as it meanders through quiet woods and meadows. Anyone taking the steam train from Haverthwaite to Lakeside can enjoy the spectacular scenery as it unfolds on either side of the track. The Lakeside and Haverthwaite Railway run five working

steam locomotives and eight coaches as well as having seven other engines on exhibition. All are lovingly maintained by enthusiasts and give a nostalgic link with the past.

A mile north or so from Newby Bridge on a back road is Finsthwaite. Its church contains a cross made from a plank cut from a pontoon bridge over the River Piave in Italy and a communion cup made from a shell. These were made for the then vicar who was an army padre in Northern Italy towards the end of World War I. In Finsthwaite churchyard lies the Polish Princess Clementina Johannes Sobieska Douglas. Tradition has it that she was the daughter of Bonnie Prince Charlie, but there does not seem to be any record of him visiting her when he stayed at Kendal. No doubt he had more urgent matters on his mind at the time.

At Lakeside the link with the past can be continued by a cruise of about 1¼ hours to Ambleside in one of Sealink's fleet of four venerable steamships, all named after birds — *Swan, Swift, Teal* and *Tern.* Charming old ladies — the *Tern* was built in 1891, but all are beautifully maintained and in perfect condition fit to continue plying the length of Windermere for many more years. All the ships have licensed refreshment bars as well as catering for younger needs.

The 10½ miles of Lake Windermere make it the longest in England. It is a lake of many faces. Once it was the preserve of wealthy industrialists who built their elegant homes along its banks, houses which are now converted into fine hotels or centres such as Brockhole owned by the Lake District National Park. Waterborne activities of all kinds which take place on the lake range from canoeing, sailing, pleasure cruising and rowing right through to waterskiing and power boats, which all manage to exist amicably side by side. So popular are power boats that nowadays speed restrictions are in force. Long straight stretches of deep water

View from the north end of Belle Isle, Windermere

1 Heald Wood
2 Dunmail Raise, Loughrigg Fell (below)
3 Nab Scar
4 Low Pike
5 Fairfield

6 Rydal Head
7 Dove Crags
8 Wansfell
9 Caudale Moor, Hen Holme Isle
   (below)

make the lake ideal for power boat racing and national events take place from time to time.

Despite its length Windermere only has a handful of islands. All the smaller ones are owned by the National Park as Access Land, but Belle Isle, the home of the Curwen family, is a 38-acre paradise with the first completely round house ever built in England. Belle Isle was named after Isabella Curwen who bought it in 1776 for £1,700 complete with its round house. It was a bargain even for those days as the original owner had spent £5,000 building the house, but sold it after his friends ridiculed the design. The island with its garden walks and the house are open to the public and a boat service operates from the landing opposite Bowness-on-Windermere car park.

Belsfield Hotel below Bowness on the lakeside has a link with the opulence of the Victorian era. Originally it was the home of a German Baron, but in 1860 it was bought by Henry William Schneider, the chairman of Barrow Steelworks and Shipyard which is now part of the Vickers group of companies. Schneider believed in living in a grand style. Each morning when he left Bowness to travel to his

office in Barrow, he would be preceded to his steam launch *Esperance* waiting at the jetty, by his butlers and staff carrying his breakfast on silver salvers. Once comfortably seated he would enjoy his meal while the launch carried him down the southern half of Windermere to Lakeside to board his personal railway coach. The train never left on its journey to Barrow before Schneider was on board and seated comfortably, but it is small wonder as he owned the railway as well. *Esperance* was built on the Clyde and transported to Barrow-in-Furness and then brought by train to Lakeside. The doubletrack railway had to be specially singled under the bridges to let her through! She is now at the Windermere Steamboat Museum, although without her unique steam engines, after being salvaged from 20 ft of water.

Bowness-on-Windermere with its jetties lined with rowing boats for hire and landing stages for the lake steamer cruises can become quite congested during the summer, especially at weekends. Try to visit out of season, say May or September to really appreciate the delights of the Windermere scene. The view on to Belle Isle is especially attractive in late spring. About ten minutes

10 Rough Holme Isle
11 High Street
12 Froswick
13 Ill Bell, Lady Holme Isle (below)
14 Wansfell

15 Applethwaite Common
16 Orrest Head
17 Brant Fell

walk from Bowness is the Windermere Steamboat Museum which was opened in 1979 by HRH The Prince of Wales. Situated at a scenic viewpoint it houses a unique collection of Victorian and Edwardian steam launches. All are afloat, in working order and are run under steam from time to time. Pride of place in the steam section is *Dolly* built in 1850, and raised in 1962 after 60 years under water. *Dolly* is the oldest mechanically propelled boat in the world. The history of racing on Windermere is well illustrated, and represented by a racing boat from the 1920s called *Canfly*; she is powered by a Rolls Royce Hawk aero engine taken from a World War I airship, and as there is no reverse the only method of stopping is to stop the engine and wait for her to drift to a halt.

Bowness is an old town, but when the railway was built the station was sited about a mile away and the town of Windermere grew round it. Originally the line was intended to run all the way through Grasmere to Keswick, but the outcry from the poet Wordsworth and other contemporary conservationists made the railway company change its mind and the line terminated at Winder-

---

PLACES TO VISIT NEAR WINDERMERE:

Lakeside and Haverthwaite Railway
A $3\frac{1}{2}$ m standard gauge railway running along the Leven Valley from Haverthwaite to Lakeside at the southern end of Windermere. Five working steam locomotives and seven other static exhibits. Locomotives and rolling stock stored and maintained at Haverthwaite Station. Connections at Lakeside with Sealink steamers, which cruise to Bowness and Ambleside.

Belle Island, Bowness
The largest, most beautiful and only inhabited island in Windermere. The interesting Round House, built in 1774, and the garden walks are open to the public. The house contains Gillow furniture and family portraits. Boat service from Bowness Promenade.

Windermere Steam Boat Museum
Unique collection of Victorian and Edwardian steam launches, all afloat, in working order and are steamed occasionally. Craft include a 1780 sailing yacht, steam launch *Dolly*, steam yacht *Esperance*, six other steam boats, an early motor boat, and two speedboats from the 1920s and 1930s.

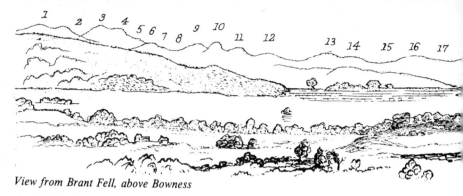

View from Brant Fell, above Bowness

1 Crinkle Crags	9 Pike o' Stickle
2 Scafell Pike	10 Harrison's Stickle
3 Bowfell	11 Pavey Ark
4 Great End	12 Blea Rigg, Silver Howe (below)
5 Great Gable	13 Tarn Crag
6 Sprinkling Crags	14 Loughrigg Fell (below)
7 Lingmoor, Skelwith (below)	15 Helm Crag (below)
8 Glaramara	16 Steel Crag

Windermere Steam Boat Museum

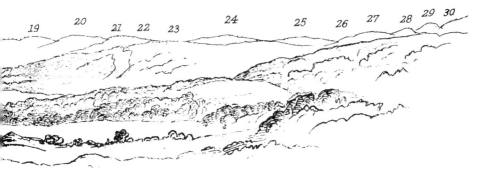

17 Skiddaw's Top
18 Nab Scar
19 Great Rigg
20 Fairfield
21 Rydal Head
22 Dove Crags
23 Wansfell Pike
24 Red Screes
25 Caudale Moor
26 Grey Crag on Hayes Water
27 High Street
28 Froswick
29 Ill Bell
30 Wansfell

Windermere Steam Boat Museum

mere. Bowness and Windermere are really two separate places, but over the years housing developments have joined them into one busy town.

Probably the finest view of Lake Windermere is from the summit of Orrest Head. To get there take the lane opposite the information centre close by Windermere station. An easy walk above Elleray Bank will bring you to a sharp right turn which eventually crosses Orrest Head. To return continue northwards and gradually zig-zag on paths towards Hag Wood then below Elleray Bank to the main road. The walk should only take an hour at the outside, but allow plenty of time to admire the view.

To the east of Windermere three valleys often escape attention. Two have motor roads that do not go over the exit passes. The most easterly is Longsleddale —a real get-away-from-it-all valley. The road follows the River Sprint up to Sedgill Farm and continues as a track over Gatescarth Pass to Hawswater and the high fells to the north. Longsleddale and

L
1½ m
1 h
*
ooo

its parallel sister valley of the Kent are rewarding places for those who prefer to leave the popular places and seek out pleasant tracks and quiet corners.

Kentmore at the road end of Kentdale is a pleasant cluster of dwellings and a good starting place for exploring the long ridges running south from the High Street range. This area is reputed to have produced giants at one time. Hugh Hird who lived at Troutbeck in Tudor times is said to have easily lifted a beam 30 feet long and 13 inches by 12 inches thick. He was able to lift this beam 6 feet off the ground into its position above the kitchen chimney at Kentmere Hall where it stays to this day.

Troutbeck valley, the most westerly of the three is a busy place with a through road climbing to more than 1,450 feet over the Kirkstone Pass. Although it is an easy challenge to modern vehicles it gives a rich panorama of views on to the high fells. The ease with which modern cars take the gradient on well metalled roads is a far cry from the days when horse

Lake steamer at Bowness Pier, Windermere

Kirkstone Pass Inn

drawn coaches made heavy work of the climb and it was then that the need for rest and shelter that the Kirkstone Pass Inn proved its worth. However let us not decry the need for refreshments even in the twentieth century for the Kirkstone is a welcome place, a real hill pub with all that the title suggests. Drive up there and walk up the steep sides of Kilnshaw Chimney before calling in at the bar. You will climb more than 1,000 feet up and the same down. A pint will taste all the better for it. Try some of their rum butter while you are there, it is a special Cumberland delicacy. The pub takes its name from a nearby rock shaped like a church steeple — hence Kirk (Church) stone.

The Romans used the valley of Troutbeck as the start for their road over the bleak fastnesses of High Street. The track up the east side of the valley over the high tops to Pooley Bridge and on to Penrith follows the line of a Roman road. Walk over here on a misty wet day and it will not be difficult to imagine you can hear the ghostly march of Roman legions. To have built a road over such high country suggests that the valleys were once dangerous places controlled by wild tribes of long ago. There is a legend that the ghosts of Bonnie Prince Charlie's army can sometimes be seen marching this way across High Street's fell tops. A suitable walk to enjoy the Troutbeck fells on a fine day starts at Troutbeck village and joins the track going north up the side of Troutbeck Valley just to the east of the campsite. Follow the track up Hall Gill to High Street, but turn left before Racecourse Hill where horse racing was held until fairly recently. Work your way round the top of Threshfield Mouth, over Stoney Cove Pike to John Bell's Banner and St Raven's Edge down to the Kirkstone Pass Inn. Careful attention to time is required if you are to reach the bar before closing time. A mile of downhill road walking towards Troutbeck and then a parallel path by way of Hird Wood will bring you back to civilisation. The

H
1m
1½h
***
oo

H
14m
6h
**
ooo

Tranquil moorings, Windermere

'township' of Troutbeck is passed by the modern motor road and it is all the better for it. Its medieval chapel, with collection shovels instead of the more prosaic boxes was rebuilt in the sixteenth century and enlarged in 1736. Burne-Jones the pre-Raphaelite artist is responsible for the design of the east window. At the south end of the village is Townend, an early seventeenth-century farm house with fine old yew trees guarding its gateway.

M
5m
2½h
**
oo

A pleasant couple of hours or so can be spent climbing Wansfell Pike from Troutbeck. Start almost opposite the Mortal Man Inn and follow Nanny Lane upwards. After about half a mile continue right with walls on either side and gradually the lane gives way to a track leading to a peak at 1,597ft. Sharp left here along a rough ridge leads to the top of Wansfell Pike. A left turn down hill marked by stakes leads on to join Nanny Lane again and back to Troutbeck. This short walk can often be used when cloud covers the high fells and has the attraction of offering views of the length of Windermere as well as northward to the high tops.

The fine landscaped gardens which surround the Cheshire Foundation nursing home of Holehird on the road between Troutbeck and Windermere are open to the public. The main gardens are maintained by Cumbria County Council and the Lakeland Horticultural Society have a splendid alpine garden and an extensive collection of heathers, rare trees and shrubs.

Back to Windermere and close to White Cross Bay caravan park in Crag Woods are a number of rocks inscribed with a whole series of curious statements and names. The inscriptions are the result of six years' labour in the early 1800s by John Longmire. The poor man was mentally deranged and had a political fixation. One rock reads 'National Debt £800,000,000. Save My Country Heaven, George and William Pitt.' One cannot

PLACES OF INTEREST NEAR TROUTBECK AND AMBLESIDE:

Townend (National Trust), Troutbeck village, 3m south east of Ambleside. A fine farmhouse built about 1626, containing carved woodwork, books, papers, domestic utensils and furniture belonging to the same yeoman family who lived there for over 300 years until 1944.

Holehird on Troutbeck-Windermere road
The gardens surround a Cheshire Foundation nursing home and include spacious lawns, rockeries, stream and pond, and many uncommon trees and shrubs. Superb views across Windermere. Also the 3-acre gardens of the Lakeland Horticultural Society, with a splendid Alpine garden, a remarkable collection of heathers and many unusual trees, shrubs and plants.

Lake District National Park Centre, Brockhole, on A591 between Windermere and Ambleside, 2½m from Bowness
The gardens and grounds overlooking Windermere have superb views, with a short nature walk along the lake shore. The house was built in the late nineteenth century as a Manchester business man's country house, and is now a National Park Centre. Exhibitions show the history of the Lake District from prehistoric times to the present, give full details of the geology and landscape, natural history and conservation problems. There are daily talks and films on a wide range of Lakeland topics.

Stagshaw Gardens, Ambleside
Mainly shrubs, trees and bulbs, many modern rhododendrons, lake views. Best in spring and early summer.

White Craggs Gardens, Clappersgate, Ambleside
Rock garden, rhododendrons, azaleas, alpine plants.

Bridge House, Ambleside

help but wonder what he would have said had he known about the many billions of pounds regularly spent by later governments.

The Lake District National Park Centre at Brockhole is unique amongst all the National Parks in Britain. Brockhole with its easy access from the A591 and a short distance from Windermere town is a visitor centre offering a wide range of exhibitions and advice to everyone from the casual visitor to students of the many facets of lakeland life and industry. Set amidst magnificent gardens and extensive grounds it offers an almost non stop audio-visual programme of talks and slide shows to cater for the interests of everyone of all ages. Foreign visitors are helped by occasional lectures in German and French languages. Regular lake shore walks and tours of the grounds and gardens are organised.

L
3½ m
2h
∗
ooo

There is a footpath walk from just below Brockhole on the A591 to Ambleside taking in Town End below Troutbeck, and then on to Ambleside by way of High Skelghyll and Jenkyn's Crag in Dovenest Wood and down to Windermere at the Ambleside landing stage. The northern terminus for lake steamers is the Ambleside landing stage, and this is another busy spot with a picnic site and information centre. It is a place to spend an idle hour in nearby Borrans Field watching the comings and goings of pleasure craft of all types. Beyond Borrans Field lie the excavated remains of the well sited Roman Fort of Galava. With two of its sides safely protected by water it must surely have been an easy place to defend. It was built around AD79 during the time of Roman expansion northward into Britain.

Two rivers join to fill this northern end of Windermere and are the breeding place of two highly edible freshwater species of fish, the char and the trout. The parents of both types of fish swim together the short distance upstream from the lake to spawn, but they then divide with char always taking the Brathay and trout the Rothay. Although they are two very similar rivers, it is an arrangement which appears to have been fixed long ago and appears to suit the different species. Fishing is by locally bought licence. Char is originally an arctic fish which prefer to live in the cold deep waters of Windermere and other lakes. It is considered a great delicacy and at one time was popular at court in London. As this was in the days before fast transport and refrigeration, the usual method was to bake the fish in a pie. Its meat is said to be preferable to salmon. Char fishermen must sink a long heavily weighted line which holds a number of bright metal spinners. The whole lot is pulled slowly behind a rowing boat to prevent the hooks from getting tangled with each other.

The building which excites the most interest to first time visitors (and for that matter regular visitors) to Ambleside, is the quaint Bridge House. It occupies a narrow bridge over Stock Ghyll beside the main road to Rydal and although very small it is complete with an oven on the ground floor and the upper storey is reached by an outside staircase. It was probably built in the late seventeenth century as a folly, but a local tradition says that it was built by a man who was too mean to buy land on which to build his house. Now owned by the National Trust it serves as an information centre. Another interesting feature in Ambleside is the rebuilt watermill on Stock Ghyll and is approached from North Road.

Ambleside has long been a meeting place and market town. With the rise in popularity of Lakeland as a holiday region it has gradually acquired a number of good quality clothing and mountaineering equipment shops and therefore it makes a good 'kitting out' base for anyone starting a hill holiday in this area.

A short distance along the main road

Windermere

H
10m
5½h
***
oooo

north of the town is Scandale Bridge. This can be used as the start of one of the finest high level walks in the Lake District — the Fairfield Horseshoe. From Scandale Bridge follow the public footpath through Rydal Park into Rydal Village, then above the church start to climb steeply up Lord Crags on to Heron Pike. From this point the way is reasonably clear over Great Rigg to the summit of Fairfield. Turn sharp right and cross Hart Crag and Dove Crag gradually descending in a southerly direction over High Pike and Low Pike to Low Sweden Bridge and back to Ambleside. Do not do as the writer once did and attempt the walk in atrocious weather and at the tricky turn on Fairfield discover that the compass had been left at home. It is not funny feeling your way across the upper reaches of Rydal Head in a raging blizzard! But, in good conditions this is a safe walk with only the gods for company.

Rydal Mount marks the start of William Wordsworth's country, it was here that he spent the last 37 years of his life. Part of the house is a pre-1574 farmer's cottage and the garden was landscaped by the poet. Rydal Mount is open to the public daily from March right through to mid January. Come to Rydal on a fine spring day and admire the aureate beauty of the wild daffodils in Dora's field. Often wrongly thought to be the inspiration of Wordsworth's immortalised '... host of golden daffodils', the golden host he refers to were seen by his sister Dorothy on a visit to Gowbarrow on Ullswater. So popular are Lakeland daffodils that a daffodil 'hot line' was opened in 1980 to give their admirers up-to-the-minute information on their pristine condition.

Dora's Field, Rydal

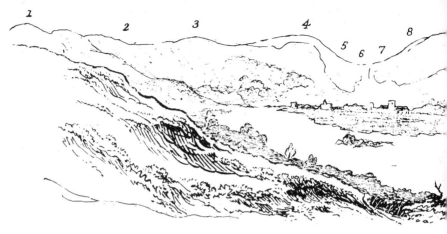

View from Silver Howe, Grasmere

1 Silver Howe
2 Serjeant Man, Easdale
3 Low White Stones
4 Steel Fell, Helm Crag (below)
5 Littledale Pike, Skiddaw
6 Raise Gap

Rydal Mount

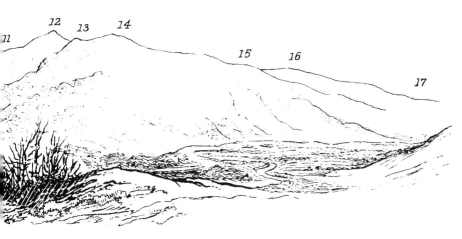

7	Great Calva in Skiddaw Forest
8	Part of Helvellyn
9	Seat Sandal
10	Dolly Waggon Pike
11	Grizedale House
12	Great Rigg
13	Greenhead Ghyll
14	Forest-side Fell
15	Nab Scar
16	Red Screes
17	Rydal Park (below)

Grasmere and Helm Crag

Below Loughrigg, Rydal

L
5½m
3h
**
oooo

Rydal Water, one of the smallest lakes, has a secluded picnic site at its head and a short woodland and riverside walk. This leads to Loughrigg Terrace with its famous panoramic view of the fells sheltering the town of Grasmere by the side of Grasmere Lake. Loughrigg Terrace can be included in the popular 'tour' of Loughrigg Fell. Paths and quiet roads complete the circuit and make an easy all-weather short day walk all the way round this miniature mountain.

At Town End to the east of Grasmere is Dove Cottage where Wordsworth lived from 1799 to 1808. The garden still bears traces of his husbandry, such as the flight of steps he and his neighbour John Fisher laid in the back garden. Together with his sister Dorothy they filled it with wild flowers gathered on the local fells and distant valleys. At first unknown, gradually Dove Cottage became the haunt of the artistic talent of the day with regular visits from such famous names as Samuel Taylor Coleridge and the essayist and opium eater Thomas de Quincey. It was de Quincey more than anyone who introduced Wordsworth's work to the world.

With the modern motor road skirting the town, Grasmere retains much of its old Cumbrian charm. The church still continues the age old custom of covering the aisle floor with rushes on the Saturday nearest 5 August. In this delightful custom the children of Grasmere come bearing rushes shaped into traditional designs; it dates from the time when the floor was of bare earth and the rush ceremony would be the annual change of covering.

The triangular field between the main road and church is where the Grasmere Sports take place very year. Sports traditionally in keeping with this hill region are fell racing, a sport of sheer spectacle, up and down steep fell sides at breakneck speeds almost matching the bravery and strength of hound trailing. Hounds are bred to follow a trail of aniseed over tough tén mile courses in amazingly fast times. Watch the fervour of locals as they bet on and argue the merits of their favourite animals. This is a real spectator sport where the atmosphere builds up to

high tension without the chance of seeing a sign of a competitor until it returns to the frantic shouts and whistles of its owner. Westmorland style wrestling is another sport unique to this area. The rules are simple. The contestants lock their arms behind each other's back and attempt to throw the opponent to the ground.

Grasmere is an ideal car-free base for the energetic walker. Set at the end of the old packhorse track from Patterdale, it makes a useful start to ascents of the Fairfield, **Dollywaggon Pike**, Helvellyn Range to the east. Nearer to base is Helm Crag with the well known landmark rocks known, according to taste, as either the 'Lion and the Lamb' or 'The Howitzer'. For the less energetic Easedale Tarn and the waterfalls of Sourmilk Gill can be visited in a short expedition beyond Goody Bridge.

A low level walk east of the main road, starts behind the Swan Hotel by way of Butter Crags to Allcock Tarn, Grey Crags and down to the Rydal Picnic site below White Moss. Cross over the stepping stones and return to Grasmere along the lakeside path.

L
$3\frac{1}{2}$m
2h
**
oo

The steep climb of the main road beyond Grasmere leads to the end of this chapter at Dunmail Raise, where the huge cairn marks the burial of King Dunmail last King of Cumberland who was slain here in a battle against the Scots in AD 945.

3 Langdale to Coniston

To the west and south of Ambleside and Windermere is a delectable area bounded on the north by Langdale and south Esthwaite and Coniston. Dozens of tiny tarns await the delight of the wandering explorer. Drive along the complex system of lanes west of Windermere and you will find your own private waterside heaven. Careful map reading will be required to find the more remote tarns, but a large number are easily accessible from public rights of way.

On the road out of Ambleside at Clappersgate the rock garden of White Craggs is open to the public. It was developed in a magnificent setting above the River Brathay by the late Charles Henry Hough out of a wooded hillside and houses a fine collection of heathers, rare shrubs and alpines from all over the world. Reginald Farrer the father of rock gardening brought plants here from his remote travels in China and Tibet. The story of the garden is beautifully told in the booklet *A Westmorland Rock Garden*. The road onward follows the River Brathay on a twisting route along the base of Loughrigg Fell to Skelwith Bridge where it divides with one road to Coniston and the other to Langdale.

The best way to enjoy the triangle made by Skelwith Force, Little Langdale Tarn and Elterwater is to get off the road and walk. It is only a short walk which could if need be, be done in a couple of hours or so, but there is so much to see it

Elterwater and the Langdale Pikes

L
5m
3h+
**
oooo

R

is best to devote most of the day to it. Start at Skelwith Bridge, where there is a bus service from Ambleside; you can either admire Skelwith Force at the beginning of the walk or save it until later, but better still look at it both in the morning and afternoon light. It is only 20 ft high but it has the greatest volume of water of any in the Lake District. Cross the bridge and a little way down the Coniston road follow a path up through the woods to the right and then by way of Park House, Elterwater Park and Low Park. Cross a minor road to High Park (follow the 1 : 25000 map carefully and the route comes easily). In the ancient wood before High Park a divergence from the track leads to the most charming Colwith Force which is almost hidden in a tree filled glen. The water falls in two leaps over a distance of 90 ft. From High Park a farm lane goes to Stang End and into Atkinson Coppice passing old slate quarries before little Langdale Tarn. Cross its outflow over the Slater's Bridge (this is a good spot for a picnic). On next by High Birk Howe and over the Wrynose-Langdale road to a wide gravel lane leading by way of Howe Banks to Elterwater and the renowned Britannia Inn. The river here is Great Langdale Beck, follow it all the way downstream past Elterwater lake to Skelwith Force and Skelwith Bridge. As previously mentioned this triangular route is a walk to linger long over and it has the advantage of refreshment stopping places at two of its three corners.

Anyone staying at Grasmere can walk over to the valley of Great Langdale by one of six or seven paths linking the two places. Chapel Stile can be said to be the proper beginning of Great Langdale and it is still rather spoilt by the debris of Thrang Slate Quarry, although small cottage and holiday home development is lately improving what was once quite an eyesore. Surely this is one answer to the opposition to holiday homes, and one cannot but question the state Chapel Stile might still be if this vogue for holiday homes had been discouraged.

Looking upstream, the right-hand wall of Great Langdale is the happy realm of climber and fell walker. The Langdale Pikes have long been the practice ground for many of Englands' expert rock climbers. Non-mountaineers can glimpse these hallowed crags after a short sharp steep climb above the New Dungeon Ghyll Hotel by way of the justly famous Dungeon Ghyll Force, then across the Stickle Ghyll and up to Stickle Tarn. This is certainly a steep walk and must not be attempted by anyone who is improperly shod. Remember that it can often be harder to climb down than up and many ankles have been damaged on this stretch of hillside!

H
2m
2h
***
oo

Stickle Tarn, as the visitor will soon realise, is not entirely natural. The local name for Stickle Ghyll is Mill Ghyll and this surely gives the clue to the reason for this tarn, which nestles in a corrie created by one of the last glaciers in Langdale. Stickle Tarn provided a head of water to power a gunpowder works which once

Cat nap at the Skelwith Stone Works

H
4m
5h
****
ooo

H
8m
7h
***
oooo

stood near Elterwater. Above the tarn is Pavey Ark, Langdale's biggest cliff. It rewards the strenuous effort of the climb up from the road when suddenly it bursts into view above the silent water of Stickle Tarn. Jack's Rake up the face of Pavey Ark is about the only time a fell walker can enter the realms of the rock climber and live to tell the tale. It follows an obvious but difficult left running crack or rake up the face of Pavey Ark. An airy place with many dangerous bits, certainly not to be attempted in anything but good weather. Anyone considering the climb should first of all consult the wealth of detail in the Pavey Ark chapter of Wainwright's *Guide to the Central Fells.*

A much safer, but still steep, way up Pavey Ark is to follow the grassy ledge which starts at the eastern end of the crag about a hundred yards up Bright Beck. Follow this ledge to the summit and perhaps start the traverse of the Langdale Pikes by way of Harrison Stickle, Loft Crag and Pike of Stickle then over Mart-

crag Moor and descend to the left by Stake Pass into Mickleden and eventually back to Langdale. The climb up is very steep but once the height is gained it is kept for the best part of the walk.

Many fellwalkers who cross the summits of the Pikes do so unaware that in crossing over the top of the steep scree gully between Loft Crag and Pike of Stickle they are passing the site of stone-age industry. Careful scrutiny will show that the scree gully is mainly filled with a greenish-grey smooth faced stone. This is a particularly hard basalt which ancient man discovered in these inhospitable surroundings and roughly shaped it into axe-heads and other cutting implements. The roughed out tools were sent down to the coast around Ravenglass for final polishing and exported examples have been noted as far away as Ireland. A short distance down the gully and on its west side is a square cave which does not take much imagination to suggest that it is probably artificial. Was this the bad

Skelwith Force in dry weather

weather shelter of our neolithic fore-fathers who worked these rock walls? How many men worked here? For how long is impossible to tell, but archaeologists have discovered that a great part of the scree in the gully is in fact waste from the stone axe factory and several factory reject implements have been found. One in the author's possession is beautifully shaped for most of its surface, apart from

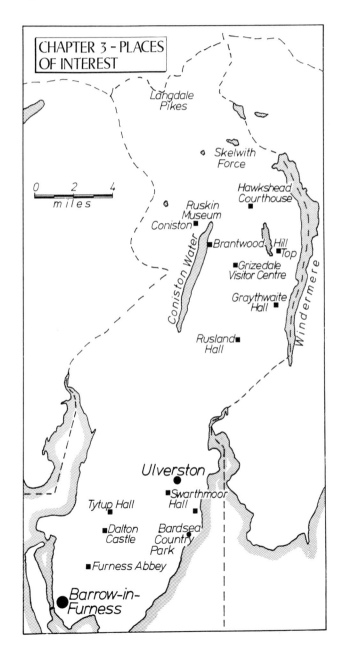

CHAPTER 3 – PLACES OF INTEREST

Langdale Pikes

Skelwith Force

Hawkshead Courthouse

Ruskin Museum

Coniston

Brantwood · Hill Top

·Grizedale Visitor Centre

Graythwaite Hall ·

Rusland· Hall

Coniston Water

Windermere

0   2   4
miles

Ulverston

·Swarthmoor Hall

Tytup Hall·

·Dalton Castle

Bardsea Country Park

·Furness Abbey

Barrow-in-Furness

The Langdale Pikes

a large flake obviously caused by the worker hitting just a little too hard. Poor man, one can imagine his disgust when he flung it down into the gulley with the rest of the scrap.

A feature when viewed from the bottom of Langdale is the huge bulk of Bowfell with the rock and grass buttress of The Band tumbling down to the junction of 'Mickleden' and Oxendale Becks above Stool End Farm. These two streams, innocent though they usually appear in summer can be full of savage power once nature takes a hand. The bridge near the old Dungeon Ghyll Hotel has been washed away more than once by floodwaters and as evidence look for the water control works on the river banks and also the piles of rock spread on flat sections of the valley floor.

H
9m
6h
***
ooo

Stool End Farm is a popular start for the route up Bowfell. The most commonly used way is to go straight up The Band and to Flat Crags and on to the Bowfell ridge. It is dreadfully steep and if it was not for the views back down Langdale the climb would be boring in the extreme. To avoid the crowds and also to follow a more exhilarating line of ascent, turn left above Stool End and follow Oxendale Beck to the footbridge above Crinkle Gill. The main path goes ahead directly to Crinkle Crag. Leave this path by turning right to follow Hell Gill and Buscoe Sike to the col with its three tarns. An easy climb due north leads to the start of Bowfell's ridge. Continue the walk northwards from Bowfell to Ore Gap with its red hematite stained rocks and soil.

There was once a proposal to build a rack railway up to Ore Gap in order to exploit the rich vein of hematite for its valuable iron content. Industrialists of the last century had a happy knack of ignoring the tremendous problems which would be encountered by such a scheme. Fortunately it was abandoned and Ore Gap remains unspoilt. Today the only problem is the way that hematite stains

our clothing, but this is a small payment where there could easily have been an ugly scar on the face of the wild crags. At Ore Gap turn right and drop steeply down to Angle Tarn, then right to follow the path down Rossett Gill to Mickleden and the Old Dungeon Gill.

Rossett Gill is one of the busiest of Lakeland foot passes, but not the most loved. Countless pairs of feet scrabbling the direct line alongside the stream have worn away the soil and vegetation and the resulting mass of loose clay and stone makes the route most unpleasant. It is unfortunate that this mess has built up, for there is a much older and far more enjoyable track down from Rossett Pass which is crying out for more constant use. This route starts at the source of the stream, but instead of following it, it angles away to the south and then by easy zig-zags beneath Bowfell to keep well away from the crowds toiling up or down the main path. In its lower reaches the old route becomes indistinct, but aim for the confluence of Rossett Gill and Stake Gill and unless they are in spate you should be able to cross dry shod over to the main path down Mickleden.

The zig-zag route from Rossett Pass is an old smugglers' path which came up from the coast near Ravenglass by way of Wasdale and the safety of the high fells. The path has other links with a past so different from the standards of today. High up on the side of Bowfell close by the path, and yet not easily seen, is a sheep fold where animals would be safely hidden in times of attack in the stormy days of border raids. Another link is the secret grave of a pack woman who perished nearby in a winter storm nearly two centuries ago. This woman regularly walked across the fells from valley to valley selling her pins and ribbons and other simple wares essential to the comfort and wellbeing of the people, who lived in what would then have been a most remote and inaccessible region.

Another route starting at Stool End and the Three Tarns Col is the delectable ridge to the south known as the Crinkle Crags. Follow the path southwards until Crinkle Crag (2,816ft) itself is crossed then ignoring any tracks which point anywhere but south-east descend to Red Tarn. Turn left and follow Browney Gill north to Oxendale Beck and back to Stool End. Close contact with the Crinkle Crags ridge will explain exactly why they are so well named. With so many undulations, by what other name could they be known?

The perfect symmetry of Pike of Blisco, known more affectionately as Pike O' Blisco, can be admired from the valley below, but it will be the faint hearted body who can resist its offer to examine its charms so close at hand. The round trip, starting and finishing at the Old Dungeon Ghyll Hotel, involves 2,000ft of climbing, but the views on a clear day make the effort more than worth while. From the hotel follow the Little Langdale

road to the bottom of the hairpin bend beyond Wall End Farm. Ascend Redacre Gill, first with it on your right hand and then cross over just beyond the stream coming down off Bleaberry Knott and continue with it on your left-hand side. This next stage is steep and rough but the angle gradually eases on to a sloping plateau with the summit in view. An easy rock scramble leads directly to the well made summit cairn. Descend by way of Red Tarn to the road by the Three Shire Stone where the old counties of Westmorland, Cumberland and Lancashire all met. Go down the road towards Little Langdale as far as the Pedder Stone (look out for the beginnings of a wall on your right of the road). A good footpath leads to Blea Tarn, then cross the Langdale road back to the Old Dungeon Ghyll Hotel and the bus to Ambleside.

It is possible to do a short climb on Pike O' Blisco from a car parked near the Three Shire Stone which only involves a little over 1,000ft of climbing.

Lakeland architecture – Blea Tarn House

Blea Tarn and the Langdale Pikes

Blea Tarn, a popular skating lake in winter, has been denuded of the forest which once surrounded it, although a clump of picturesque pines remain. Rhododendrons have taken over where once there were tall trees. The finest view of the Langdale Pikes can be found about 600ft above Blea Tarn on the slopes of Lingmoor. Climb from the gate on the Little Langdale road above Wall End, over Side Pike and then follow the wall over rough heathery slopes (hence the meaning of 'Lingmore' — the old name for heather), to the summit of Lingmoor. The best views of the Pikes will be found on the descent in the larch covered slopes above Blea Tarn House.

Leaving the high fells behind for a while we can turn our attention again to Windermere. Unlike the east bank, the western side has very little road or footpath access apart from the section below Claife Woods, and so the best way to view this bank is from the water. This does not mean, however, that there is

H
2½m
2h
**
ooo

nothing to see in the oval shaped tract of land bounded on one side by Windermere and Coniston the other. To the north are fine old mansions and in the middle a vast area of forest mostly with public access, together with a sprinkling of lakes and tarns of renowned beauty.

At the northern end of Windermere is Brathay Hall or High Brathay as it was known in the early nineteenth century when it was built for the Harden family. Nowadays the hall and grounds are used by the Brathay Outwardbound School as a training centre for young people. Wray Castle about a mile downlake is a modern castle owned by the National Trust and tenanted by the Freshwater Biological Research Association.

The area of forest bounded on the west by the Brathay-Sawrey road is mostly owned by the National Trust and gives one of the few places where the public have free access to the west bank of Windermere. A pleasant journey can be made on foot, partly across the low lying

The chain ferry across Windermere

PLACES OF INTEREST NEAR WINDERMERE (WEST BANK)

Hill Top (National Trust), near Sawrey

A seventeenth-century house, the home of Beatrix Potter, with some of her original drawings, furniture, china and pictures. Due to the small size of the house and its popularity the number of visitors may be restricted at busy times. No electric light in the house.

Hawkshead Courthouse (National Trust), north of Hawkshead village

The fifteenth-century courthouse is all that remains of the manorial buildings of Hawkshead, once held by Furness Abbey. The building now houses a museum of rural life.

Rusland Hall, north of Haverthwaite

Early Georgian mansion in an idyllic setting, containing period panelling, sculpture, furniture, paintings, clocks and watches, mechanical piano and organ, early photographic equipment. The landscaped gardens contain peacocks, specimen trees and shrubs.

Graythwaite Hall, 2 m north of Lakeside

An Elizabethan House (not open), with gardens open to the public, especially noted for azaleas, rhododendrons, and flowering shrubs.

Grizedale Forest Visitor and Wildlife Centre (Forestry Commission), 2½ m south west of Hawkshead on Satterthwaite road (336944)

There are displays showing all aspects of the forest, its geology, soils, land use, forest industries, industrial archaeology, tree nursery and wild life. There are walks and trails starting at the centre. Car parks and camp site. Parties by arrangement, write to Forestry Commission: 35 Stricklandgate, Kendal, Tel: Kendal 22587.

undulating moor, through wild forest and partly on the lakeside. Start at Far Sawrey and walk north along the forest lane by way of Moss Eccles and Wise Eens Tarns, then over Long Height to High Wray and on to High Wray Bay. Turn right and follow the shore of Windermere to Belle Grange where there is a choice of route. To turn right will take you through forest again on a path which sits on the edge of a steep slope down to the lake. Beyond is the haunted wood where a Lakeland bogle or goblin known as the 'Crier of Claife', is reputed to live and here there is a marvellous view across Windermere. This track eventually connects with a lane back to Far Sawrey. The alternative route is to continue along the shore road from Belle Grange to a point below Low Pate Crag where a path leads south westwards to join the lane to Far Sawrey. | L 4½ m 2½ h * ooo

| L 2½ m 1½ h * oo

Another walk in the forest of Claife is to climb Latterbarrow from the Hawkshead road and continue on through the forest to Long Height. Turn left along the forest road to High Wray and on to High Wray Bay. Return by field paths above Belham Tarn to Hole House and a short road walk to the foot of the Latterbarrow. | L 2½ m 1½ h * ooo

A chain ferry across the narrowest part of Windermere between Sawrey and Bowness carries on a service which is thought to have been started by the Abbot of Furness in medieval times. Certainly there was a ferry existing in the seventeenth century for the records show that there was a tragic accident with a ferry in 1635 when forty-seven people were drowned. At one time the ferry only ran during daylight hours because of a fear that the bogle who lives up on Claife Heights would come and call to the boatman. In the old days there was only one ferryman to operate the service and it was necessary for intending passengers to shout loud enough for him to hear inside the local inn. The ferryman stopped carrying night time passengers when the

Esthwaite Water

Crier of Claife called for him and kept him out on the lake all through a wild and stormy night. For generations afterwards any hopeful night passengers shouted themselves hoarse without tempting the ferryman from the warmth of the local bar.

The road from the ferry towards Esthwaite Lake passes through the picturesque villages of Far Sawrey and Near Sawrey. Hill Top at Near Sawrey was the home of one of the greatest benefactors to the National Trust in the Lake District. This was the home of Mrs William Heelis, better known as Beatrix Potter, whose delightful animal stories are mostly set in the Lakes. Tom Kitten lived at Hill Top and Squirrel Nutkin sailed across Derwentwater on a raft. Pigling Bland had a most difficult time when he crossed over from Lancashire to Westmorland by mistake. It was from royalties on her books that Beatrix Potter was able to buy up large tracts of woodland and fells which are now in trust to the nation. Hill Top, where she wrote a number of her books, is a seventeenth-century farm house and contains a number of Beatrix Potter's original drawings, as well as a collection of china and furniture. The house is open during daylight hours from April to the end of October, but owing to its small size and the popularity of its late owner, it can get rather crowded, so the best time to visit is away from the more busy times or seasons.

Esthwaite Water has a charm all its own especially when the water lilies are in bloom. There is something about its position which conveys a feeling of solitary calm and serenity. Beyond its northern end is the oval shaped tarn of Priest's Pot, called by that name because it is supposed to hold enough liquid to satisfy a priest's thirst. The quiet lanes and forest tracks around Esthwaite Water are ideal for horse riding and pony trekking, sports well catered for by several stables in the locality.

Beyond the lake we come to the ancient

View from near Tent Lodge on east bank of Coniston Water

1	Knot End	5	High Fell
2	Walna Scar	6	Keld Gill Head
3	Coniston Old Man	7	Wetherham
4	Buckbarrow, copper mines (below)	8	Yewdale Fells

town of Hawkshead which became a central market in the Middle Ages for the scattered inhabitants of the wild regions beyond Windermere. The monks of Furness Abbey, with interests in sheep rearing, built Hawkshead Hall to the north of the town but now only the courthouse remains. Fortunately it is still in a fine state of preservation, and it now houses a museum of local rural life as lived over a hundred years ago. At one time a stream flowed down the middle of Flag Street in Hawkshead, and was used as an open sewer. The stream is now covered over, but the town remains a muddle of delightful nooks and corners.

Here is another link with Wordsworth who attended Hawkshead Grammar School, where from all accounts he spent several very happy years and it was during his weekends and holidays he first grew to love the fells and tarns of Lakeland.

A short walk taking in all the delights of Hawkshead starts by the church, crosses fields past the vicarage, through the parkland of Keen Ground and on to the road below Hawkshead Courthouse. The return is by a path, running south east from Hall Bridge to Colthouse and back by lane and road to Hawkshead over Pool Bridge with distant views across Esthwaite Water.

To the east and south of Esthwaite lies Grizedale Forest where by careful planning the Forestry Commission have opened up huge areas of woodland to public access. They have laid out two forest trails, one long (The Silurian Way) and one short (Millwood). Both are properly waymarked and easy to follow, but for the more adventurous there are several routes or rights of way throughout the forest. One of the many signposted features on the Silurian Way is the remains of an old 'Bloomery' where hematite was smelted into iron using locally made charcoal.

One of the features of this forest is the Visitor and Wildlife Centre where there is a permanent exhibition of forestry work and a tree nursery. Nature trails and short waymarked walks are laid out and are so popular that booking is often

L
$1\frac{1}{2}$ m
1 h
*
ooo

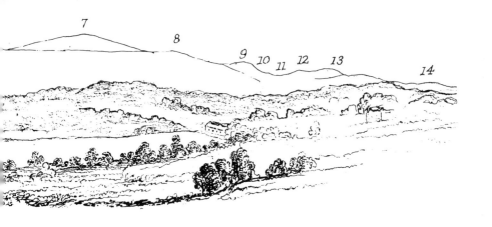

9 High Fell
10 Calf Crag, Yewdale and Tilberthwaite
   (below)
11 Lingmoor, Langdale
12 Raven Crag

13 Oxen Fell
14 Dovecrags, Hartsop

essential for large parties, but there should be no problem for the occasional visitor who wants to learn about one of the more accessible forests. The intimate Theatre in the Forest was opened in 1970 with seating for 229. Throughout the season it offers events ranging from drama, orchestral concerts to film shows. Bookings can be made by telephoning Satterthwaite 291.

Meandering lanes from Grizedale lead by way of Satterthwaite towards Windermere and Graythwaite Hall standing in a sheltered fold above the lake. The Elizabethan house is not open to the public, but the grounds are and the best time to visit these is in May when the display of azaleas and rhododendrons are at their best.

Before returning to the higher fells a visit to the early Georgian Manor of Rusland is recommended. Rusland is three miles north of Haverthwaite on the Grizedale road. The house is set in landscaped gardens with peacocks roaming freely. Inside are several interesting and unusual items including mechanical pipe organs and a grand piano which plays itself. There is also a collection of vintage photographic equipment.

In the north-west corner above Coniston is one of the most photographed views in England, the ever popular Tarn Hows. Park your car above Howgraves and look northwestwards to Langdale across the islands dotted with bright red rhododendrons in May and June and admire the majestic skyline of rolling fells. This is one of the most charming faces of Lakeland. To really get the feel of Tarn Hows follow the path around the lake. It is only about 1½ miles all round, but the surroundings should keep all but the most unobservant happy for as long as time permits. The walk can easily be extended southwards to take in a view from the northern end of Coniston Lake. This extension starts from the most westerly of the Tarn Hows car parks and goes south through Hill Fell Plantation and down to the road by Monk Coniston. Return by walking up the Hawkshead road for about a half mile and follow the path through Burnt Intake Woods, pas-

L
1½m
1h
*
oooo

L
2m
1h
**
ooo

53

sing Wharton Tarn on the right. Turn left at the road and then back to another viewing session above Tarn Hows.

The long straight sheltered water of Coniston make it the ideal place for attempts on the water speed records. Probably the most famous attempt was that by the late Sir Donald Campbell who died tragically one morning in a cloud of spray when his boat, the Bluebird, somersaulted after either hitting a submerged log or becoming airborne. No one ever really knew what happened.

As with Windermere, the motorist must keep to the east side of Coniston Water if he wants to drive close to the water's edge. The road from the northern end hugs the shore for most of its way down to Water Yeat where it joins the A5084. About a quarter of a mile west of the car park at the top (northern) end of the lake is a circular clump of overgrown trees and undergrowth. The clue of what this is, or more correctly was, is shown on the large scale 1 : 25000 map of the area. This is the Labyrinth and was once a well tended maze, but now it is very much overgrown through time and neglect.

Down the east side of the lake for just a little over a mile is the beautifully situated house called Brantwood once the home of John Ruskin, Victorian environmentalist, artist and writer. Spring is the best time to come here as the gardens are then a mass of daffodils and azaleas and rhododendrons.

A path which starts opposite Low Bank Ground Farm halfway between the head of the lake and Brantwood leads up through the forest to Pen Intake beneath Crag Head. It gradually gains height until it re-enters forest and passes Lawson Park. Turn right here and either walk down the cart track, or better still find the path down through Machell Coppice to the lakeside. Return by road and perhaps include a visit to Brantwood on the way back.

L
5 m
2½ h
**
oo

From High Nibthwaite at the southern end of Coniston Water follow the gently rising forest above Water Park. Look out for a path off to the right which will lead to the Top O'Selside. Continue to the right past Arnsbarrow Tarn and Neile Stove Crag then down the valley to High Bethecar. Turn right, away from the house and back to High Nibthwaite.

M
3½ m
2h
**
oo

The A5084 is a busy road in the season, but it does give access to the west side of the lake before going inland to Torver and on to Coniston village. Opposite the car park and picnic site beyond Browne Howe at the bottom end of Coniston Water a track climbs northwest into the jumble of crags and fells of Torver Low Common. A little way above Black Beck turn left on the path zig-zagging westwards and then north to Greave Ground. Turn right along the lane to Hazel Hall and right again to either of the two paths which turn south just before Beck Stones. Follow the path past Bloomery Tarn and across Tottle Bank back to the track leading down to the lakeside car park. The bloomery shown beyond the tarn is

L
6 m
3h
**
ooo

PLACES OF RUSKIN INTEREST:

Brantwood, east bank of Coniston Water
The home of John Ruskin from 1872 to 1900 and contains pictures by Ruskin and contemporary artists, Ruskin's furniture, part of his library, his boat and coach. One of the most beautifully situated houses in Lakeland, fine gardens and interesting nature trails. Temporary exhibitions in the converted coach house.

Ruskin Museum, Yewdale Road, Coniston
Displays the life and work of John Ruskin, as well as local history, scenery, industries and mineral specimens.

the site of ancient iron production from local hematite.

L
4½ m
2h
*
oo

Another walk around here is the round of Torver Common which takes in a stretch of lakeside footpath. Start in Torver village and follow the old abandoned railway track for about 200 yd, turn right on the path by Grass Guards, then down to the lake by way of Torver Common Woods. Turn right along the lake shore and walk to the road at Sunny Bank. Right here to Mill Bridge where a track on the left follows Torver Beck into Torver village.

Man has lived around Coniston since time immemorial, as a quick look on the map of the moorland to the west of the town will show. Torver High Common is liberally dotted with remains of hut bases, ancient cairns and stone circles of ancient man. One can only conjecture at the reason for standing stones and circles, but the most plausible explanation offered to date is that they were part of a sophisticated calendar system. In days before written records it must surely have been necessary to have some means of recording the passing of time, for how else would these people have known when to plant their crops. As we know only too well there is often a mild spell followed by cold weather early in the year. This could prove fatal to anyone planting crops too early, hence the early need for some form of calendar to record the passing of the seasons. The moorland south of the Walna Scar road is an eerie place dotted with cairns and stone circles and so it is not difficult to believe reports that a flying saucer has been sighted over Little Arrow Moor!

Coniston village, like Ambleside and Keswick, is a popular place for shopping and gazing at its old cottages and churches. It has all the requirements of a tourist village, with an information centre, car parking facilities and several hotels and cafes. It grew to its present size in the heyday of copper mining and quarrying when the mineral content of the surrounding hills was being exploited. Today it makes a useful base from which to climb the Old Man of Coniston, or to go sailing or cruising on the lake. There is a public launching site beyond the Cat Bank car park and the Lake District National Park hire out boats and sailing dinghies from here. Fishing, as on most of the other lakes, is good and a licence is necessary, but can be purchased locally.

Although Coniston Old Man is one of the most climbed peaks in Britain, most of the ways up are a positive slog, but if you include it in a round tour of the fells as will shortly be described then the effort is well spent. The view from the summit cairn, or 'Man' encompasses the whole of Morecambe Bay and even Northern Ireland and Scotland on a clear day. The majestic grandeur of the Lakeland Fells spread out to the north and east, is positively breathtaking. Most visitors who climb Coniston Old Man do so by following the Walna Scar and quarry roads from beyond the railway station. This can be tedious and the best route is to start at the Sun Hotel on a path which climbs along the south bank of Church Becks. Do not cross over at Miners' Bridge but continue upwards until the quarry road is met at its last bend, before climbing steeply up through the old slate quarry. A well used path leads from the top of the quarry to the summit. Having gained the 2,633 ft to the top of the 'Old Man', rather than descend by the way you have come up, why not continue around the grand horseshoe to Wetherlam? The turf covered ridge is a positive delight to the feet across Brim Fell and you could shorten the walk by dropping down Coppermines Valley from Swirl How and Levers Water, but the little extra effort involved in climbing Wetherlam makes all the difference.

H
8m
5h
***
ooo

The descent from Wetherlam into Levers Water Beck passes literally dozens

Yew Tree Farm, Coniston

of open shafts and tunnels. These are the visible surface remains of intensive copper mining which was carried on here until cheaper imported metal undercut local industry. **On no account should the workings be entered as they are all in a dangerous state. Steer well clear of the shafts** as often as not the surface rock is covered with small rounded stones just waiting to act as roller bearings to assist the unwary to their death, take care especially in mist. The ruined buildings and spoil heaps near the youth hostel are the remains of crushing mills and smelting plant, which give an indication of the size of the industry which went on in this Coppermines Valley. The almost square shape of Levers Water makes an ideal high picnic site on a hot day. It can be visited as part of an archaeological wander through the mine workings and makes a pleasant alternative to a hard day on the high fells.

H
7½ m
4½ h
***
ooo

Another circuit to include Wetherlam is from Little Langdale by way of High Birk Howe, Low Hall Garth and the Greenburn Beck, then left steeply up Wetherlam Edge to Swirl How and Prison Band. At Swirl How turn right and return across Great Carrs to Wet Side Edge. Do not go on to the Wrynose road but turn right over Rough Crags and down to Greenburn Beck and retrace your steps to Little Langdale.

The ancient town of Ulverston, with its market house dating from 1736 and an even older church, is a useful place to visit on a day when the clouds are down in the high valleys. Often the weather has remained kind around this end of Furness when it is wet in the central areas. Cumbria Crystal in Lightburn Road is a modern glassworks and visitors are allowed to watch craftsmen at work blowing and forming glassware. It is usual to visit by an appointment made by telephoning Ulverston 54400. Ulverston is connected to the sea by a short canal and at Guides House, Canal Foot, lives

PLACES TO VISIT NEAR FURNESS:

Conishead Priory, Ulverston
Victorian Gothic house with fine decorative plaster ceilings, marble fireplaces and wood panelling. Gardens and woods. Buddhist College.

Swarthmoor Hall, Ulverston
An Elizabethan house with mullioned windows, oak staircase and panelled rooms. The birthplace of Quakerism when George Fox lived there, and still belongs to the Society of Friends.

Tytup Hall, Dalton-in-Furness
Small seventeenth- and eighteenth-century house with original painted panelling.

Dalton Castle (National Trust), Dalton-in-Furness
Fourteenth-century pele tower

Furness Abbey (Dept of Environment), between Barrow and Dalton
Extensive ruins of a red sandstone abbey started in 1127, which by the dissolution was very wealthy — the second richest Cistercian house in England.

Furness Museum, Ramsden Square, Barrow-in-Furness
Stone Age, Bronze Age and Iron Age material, local ship models (including important makers' models). Travelling and contemporary exhibitions.

Mr Alf Butler who is the guide to the route across Cartmel Sands. This lesser known crossing is of similar age to the Morecambe Bay route and like that one it saved a considerable road journey in pre-turnpike road days. Anyone wishing to cross Cartmel Sands should contact Mr Butler beforehand.

Two or three miles north of Ulveston is the Haybridge Nature Reserve at Greenodd for red deer and other wild life.

Greenodd, the last place on the Langdale — Coniston itinerary, was once a ship building town, but it never became another Barrow and its only claim to nautical fame was an experimental sailing vessel aptly named the *Elephant*. The boat was shaped like a square box with identical bow and stern, the bowspit was removable and could be used at either end. Greenodd had links with sea faring from way back and its very name 'Greenoddi' comes from old Norse.

4 Eskdale to Wasdale

The wedge of country bounded on the east by the Coniston Fells and on the northwest by Ennerdale contains some of the best, and at the same time least known, mountains and valleys of Lakeland. The central giants radiating from Scafell are known to thousands, but how well known is Pillar mountain? Most of the lesser known valleys are here as well, valleys that by their apparent inaccessibility make them all the more interesting to the discerning tourist. These valleys have ancient farmsteads which have been owned by the same families for generations. It takes time to explore these southwestern valleys and fells, but the time is well spent.

Without a doubt the most beautiful valley of them all is the Duddon, which starts above the Three Shires Stone on Wrynose Pass where the boundaries of Lancashire and Cumberland meet with Westmorland. In its journey to the golden sands of its estuary, the River Duddon flows between a pageant of wild flowers; wood anemones, violets, primroses bloom beneath the boughs of mountain ash trees where later masses of bluebells create a mist in their season. Spring is the most delightful time for the visitor to the Duddon. In all the length of its valley there is only one village, this is the tiny hamlet of Ulpha. Its church, a typical dale chapel, has a set of wall paintings which were uncovered in 1934. The old hall is a ruined sixteenth-century pele tower in the ravine of Holehouse Gill. There is a waterfall in the gill known as 'Lady's Dub', where the traditional story is of a woman who was drowned here while fleeing from a wolf.

Three-quarters of a mile below the village of Ulpha, is the site of ancient iron workings (marked on the Ordnance Survey map as 'Bloomery') and can be visited by a footpath which climbs to the southeast across the side of Great Stickle and then down to Hovel Knott and Pickthall Ground Farm. Turn right here and return to the Duddon road by Thick Wood.

L 3m 1½h ** oo

If you want to walk on fells where you are hardly ever likely to see another person all day, then the fells on either side of the Duddon Valley are the places to visit. Climb up Dow Crag for instance and there will probably be only a handful of fell walkers on its summit, but across the other side of Goats Water, Coniston Old Man will be positively crowded. The packhorse road across Walna Scar starts at Seathwaite Bridge and climbs up along the south side of Long House Gill. At the col between Walna Scar and Brown Pike turn left and cross the latter and then on to Dow Crag itself. Return by dropping down to Goats Hause and down to Seathwaite Tarn. Follow the path on the south side of Seathwaite Tarn reservoir until you meet the reservoir road which makes an easy descent back to the Walna Scar Road and Seathwaite Bridge.

H 7m 3½h *** ooo

Still in the upper reaches of the Duddon Valley the almost perfect symmetry of Harter Fell invites exploration. The most commonly used route is from Eskdale, but the one from Birks Bridge in Duddon is a worthy alternative. From the car park by Hinning House Close cross over the arched Birks Bridge and on to Birks. An easy cart track through the forest leads to Grassguards. Turn right and walk up Grassguards Gill towards the col between Grassguards and Spothow Gills. At the highest point turn to the right and follow a ruined wall to the

H 4m 2½h *** ooo

summit of Harter Fell. Return by the short and well trodden path direct to Birks and on to the car park.

M
3½ m
2 h
***
ooo

Hinning House car park can also be used as a base for several short walks across the low fells to the east of Seathwaite Tarn. Take the track southwards from the car park over Pike How and Foss How then across Tarn Beck by the stepping stones. On to Crag Band, but not quite as far as the reservoir road, and turn right towards High Tongue across Tarn Beck. A sharp right turn up to Worm How and down to the road for a quarter of a mile or so to the National Trust land of The Hows, where another path leads back to the car park. This walk can be shortened by using either of the tracks which diverge around Brow Side.

H
5½ m
3 h
***
oo

Still moving back upstream, there is a walk starting at Cockley Beck Bridge close by the junction of the Wrynose and Hardnott roads. The walk follows a path alongside Cockley Beck up to the top of Grey Friar and returns by Great Carrs, Hell Gill Pike and Wet Side Edge to the Three shire Stone at Wrynose. Turn left down the road then leave it by turning

Three Shire Stone, Wrynose

right on to a path which follows the river Duddon through Wrynose Bottom and back to Cockley Beck Bridge. This point can also be used as the base for the steep climb up to Crinkle Crags by way of Gaitscale Close. Walk as far along the Crags as you fancy, but it will be necessary to retrace your steps and then return to the top of Wrynose by crossing Cold Pike and Rough Crags. From Wrynose the route follows the road and path by Wrynose Bottom.

H
8 m
4 h
***
ooo

The minor road southwards down the valley towards Duddon Bridge is hardly built for fast driving, but who should want to travel at speed in such a delectable spot? At Duddon Bridge the sudden transition as you join the A595 comes as a shock after the quiet of the Duddon Valley, but at least it leads on to other delights. Why not stop and climb a little fell which rises 1,970 ft in just over two miles from sea level. This is Black Combe, which can be climbed from Whicham Mill alongside the little stream between Black and White Combes. Turn left along the edge of the combe to the summit. Return the same way as far as the col but continue to Stoupdale Crags and then sharp right across the broad ridge of White Combe and back to the main road above Whicham Mill.

H
7 m
3½ h
***
oo

On the narrow coastal plain between the estuaries of the Duddon and the Esk is Millom, an ancient town with a ruined castle now partly occupied by a farm house. Millom manages to retain its ancient atmosphere despite the iron ore workings nearby. The Folk Museum in St George's Road features the history of iron production from mining through to smelting, and local miners have built a replica of a shaft inside the museum. There is also a smithy and an old miner's cottage nearby. Other features of the museum include relics of peat working, agriculture and other local industries.

Further round the coastal plain from Millom is Bootle — a town in complete contrast with its namesake near Liverpool. Wordsworth once came here for a seaside holiday, and certainly the sunset views across the Irish Sea towards the Isle of Man can be quite stunning. Three minor roads connect the Esk and Duddon and the most famous is that across the so-called difficulties of Hard Knott. It is a steep road and on a busy day can be a nightmare for AA patrolmen. If you are towing a caravan and the roads look like being crowded then avoid Hard Knott, but on any other occasion and without encumbrance the road has few difficulties if taken carefully.

At the bottom of Hard Knott is the well sited Roman fort of Hard Knott Castle or Mediobogdum as they knew it. The fort has been extensively excavated with some rebuilding of the outer walls, and it does not need a military strategist to realise the defensive potential of this site, which commands the route from the Roman sea port of Ravenglass over the wild fells to Ambleside and onto Carlisle and Hadrians Wall. Mediobogdum was an important garrison fort and it is not difficult to picture the legionaries drilling on the parade ground just above the fort.

H
15m
9h+
★★★★
○○○○

From the valley bottom by Brotherikeld is the start of the longest and one of the toughest walks in Lakeland. This is the ascent of Scafell Pikes by way of the valley of the Esk. The route lies across Brock Crag and Rowantree Crags to Silvery Bield Crag then down by way of Sampson's Stones to How Beck, which is followed straight up to Mickledore. A right turn across the boulder slope leads to the top of Englands highest fell — Scafell Pike. The return route continues on across the rough jumble of rocks to Esk Hause where a sharp right turn leaves the main track and down to the infant River Esk which is followed all the way back to Brotherikeld. It cannot be stressed too much that this is a long hard walk only to be undertaken by the fittest walkers and then only on days when there

is a minimum of nine or ten hours good daylight. The walk can be shortened slightly by omitting the rough ground from Broad Crag to Esk Hause, and descending by turning right at Broad Crag col and following Little Narrowcove to the River Esk.

As an alternative to the intense activity required in following the last climb, a whole series of short easy valley bottom walks can be devised by wandering along the many paths radiating from Brotherikeld. The name of the farm is from Old Norse with Keld meaning 'a farm in the valley bottom'. An easier mountain walk nearby is to follow the Harter Fell track starting at the bottom of the Hard Knott road. Instead of climbing Harter continue on across the col and then turn right to Green Crag and over Silver How to Torn Crag and down to the river by Low Birker Farm. Follow the path upstream from Doctor Bridge and back to the starting point at the Hardnott road.

L
2/3
1/2
★★
○○○

H
6m
3h
★★
○○

The Woolpack Inn at Boot is a reminder of the commerce of days long ago when it provided a resting place for both pack ponies and their leaders, when they were carrying loads of wool across the fells to the port of Whitehaven. Above Boot is the start of a track leading up the valley of Whillan Beck to Burnmoor Tarn just over half way to Wasdale. On the return leg of this easy walk turn left across Whillan Beck at Lambford Bridge and follow the contours round by Eel Tarn back to Boot by way of the Woolpack Inn.

M
6½
3h
★★
○○○

Just outside Boot is Dalegarth Station, the upper terminus of the fifteen-inch gauge Ravenglass & Eskdale Railway or 'Ratty' as it is affectionately known. The railway, of just under seven miles, was originally built in 1875 as a standard gauge track to carry iron ore (and later passengers) from Nab Gill mines near Boot down to the main line at Ravenglass. The line was never a commercial proposition and was eventually closed in

Ravenglass and Eskdale Railway

1913. In 1915 Mr W. J. Bassett-Lowke the famous model engineer took over the line and converted it to the fifteen-inch gauge it is today. He did this mainly to test his model steam locomotives, but early on in the narrow gauge life of the line an attempt was made to provide an attractive and commercial service. The line saw many troublesome ups and downs but in 1961 The Ravenglass and Eskdale Railway Preservation Society took over the line and began to build up the rolling stock of steam and diesel locomotives and both open and saloon coaches. This popular attraction makes an ideal family day out and the line can also be used as a novel means of transport at the beginning or end of walks in Eskdale. There is a footpath map by the road outside Dalegarth station and passengers leaving the train at Dalegarth, even if they have only an hour or so to spare, can best use it with a visit to the nearby woodland glen near Dalegarth Hall. At the end of a short zig-zag track through the woods is the beautiful 60 ft-high waterfall of Stanley Force. The best way to reach Stanley Force after leaving Dalegarth station is to turn right and walk a little way along the road and then turn left along a signposted track to cross over the River Esk. Turn left before Dalegarth Hall towards Stanley Gill which is followed uphill to the waterfall. Return by the same route. Try to make a short diversion on the return by turning right at Dalegarth Hall and walk upstream to visit Gill Force, it will only add another twenty minutes or so to the walk.

For anyone with an afternoon to spare the Stanley Force walk can be extended by first of all keeping on the left bank of the river and visiting Gill Force on the way out, then walking upstream along the Esk as far as Doctor Bridge. Cross over here onto the other bank and walk downstream to Lower Birker. About a quarter of a mile further on take the left fork in the track and climb to just beneath Hartley Crag, where another path

L
4m
2h
*
oooo

L
5½m
2½h-
**
oooo

Ravenglass and Eskdale Railway (The 'Ratty'), Ravenglass to Dalegarth
Originally, from 1875 to 1913, a 7 mile branch line from the Furness Railway for iron ore. Converted to 15 in gauge in 1915, now carries tourists, mainly using steam locomotives and saloon and open coaches.

Muncaster Mill, 1 m north east of Ravenglass
A water-powered cornmill on the River Mite, built in the late eighteenth century, which milled flour until World war I and cattle feed and oatmeal until 1954. The mill and 13 ft overshot waterwheel have been restored and show the process of milling to the visitor. Trains from the Ravenglass and Eskdale Railway stop at the mill if required.

Muncaster Castle, Ravenglass
Built on the site of a Roman tower, there is a fourteenth-century pele tower with fifteenth- and nineteenth-century additions. On display are sixteenth- and seventeenth-century furniture, pictures, embroidery, porcelain and tapestries. Landscaped gardens with ornamental shrubs, birds and animals.

Calder Hall Nuclear Power Station, Seascale
There are five nuclear reactors at the power station and the Windscale reprocessing plant (on the same site). Calder Hall was the first nuclear power station in Britain, opened in 1956. Visits to the reactors and turbine hall can be arranged **if booked well in advance**.

Millom Folk Museum, St George's Road, Millom
Displays of local life, agriculture and industry, especially iron mining and smelting. Replica of a miner's cottage kitchen, blacksmith's forge and underground iron ore mine.

leads off down to the right and into Dalegarth Hall Woods. Return to Dalegarth by way of Esk View and Brook House.

In the middle of little visited Ulpha Fell, and set in a wild and beautiful situation is Devoke Water. This offers quiet sanctuary away from bustle and crowds; it is famous among anglers for the red trout which were supposed to have been introduced in the Middle Ages by the monks of Furness Abbey. To get to Devoke Water drive along the main road to Ulpha as far as a little stream beyond Pike How. Leave the car here and walk along an easy track to this least known of Lakeland tarns. To make a round trip do not return by the same route but take the track to Woodend and back to the road at Wood End Bridge. Turn right along the road for a short distance until you see a track off to the left. Follow this across Sike Moss to just before Birkerthwaite Farm, when another left turn follows an easy path back to the car.

The only other village in the whole length of the Esk is Eskdale Green where there is an Outward Bound Mountain School. The public house, the King George, has not always been known as such. Until World War I it was called the King of Prussia, but ill feeling towards all things German at that time caused it to change its name.

Above Eskdale Green in Miterdale is the ruin of a farm house which is haunted by the ghost of a gypsy who came to the place disguised as a woman. The farmer was away at the time and his wife took in her lodger in good faith. It was only when she noticed the man-sized boots on the gypsy woman's feet that she became alarmed. When the man was asleep she poured boiling tallow down his open mouth and it is said that his horrible gurglings can be still heard on moonlit nights even to this day.

In a pleasanter vein, Miterdale is a lovely place, probably one of the last

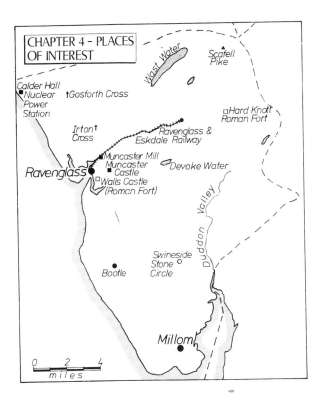

CHAPTER 4 – PLACES OF INTEREST

Scafell Pike

Wast Water

Calder Hall Nuclear Power Station

†Gosforth Cross

□Hard Knott Roman Fort

Irton† Cross

Ravenglass & Eskdale Railway

Muncaster Mill

Ravenglass

Muncaster Castle

◁Devoke Water

□Walls Castle (Roman Fort)

Duddon Valley

Swineside Stone Circle ○

Bootle •

Millom

0   2   4
miles

'unexplored' valleys in the Lake District; the River Mite starts below, but for some quirk of nature is not fed by Burnmoor Tarn. As it is with all the most interesting places the best way to explore the copses and fell sides of Miterdale is on foot.

L 6 m 3 h ** oo

From Eskdale Green take the path running north east over Brown How and then eventually down to the stream beyond Low Place. Turn left and return downstream through the woods along the farm track back to Eskdale Green. The walk can be extended beyond Low Place by following the path all the way to the head of the river and even beyond to Burnmoor Tarn. To return cross the moor and join the track descending Tongue Moor. There is a fine view of Scafell dominating the head of Miterdale.

Nearby Muncaster Fell keeps the Esk and Mite from each other until they reach the sea and this makes a good 'low level'

mountain climb. Muncaster Fell is only 758 ft high and will often be cloud free when bad weather prevents higher expeditions. The starting point as with most round tours is unimportant, but for the sake of clarity let us assume the start is from a car parked near Eskdale Green, or for that matter as a passenger alighting from the 'Ratty' at the same place. Follow the path alongside the railway and through Bankhead Wood to Rabbit How. Cut across the moor on the path behind Muncaster Head and take a low level track through Birks Plantation to High Eskholme. If you can make a full day tour, then at the chapel in Chapel Wood turn left and visit Muncaster Castle and return to the main route by the three-islanded tarn on Chapel Hill. Continue the walk across the Knobbly Summit ridge of Muncaster Fell passing the stone table of Ross's Camp back to

L 6½ m 3 h ** ooo

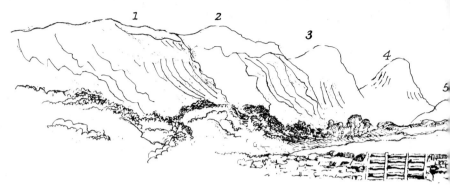

View from near Strands below Wastwater

1 *Buckbarrow Pike*	4 *Great Gable*
2 *Middle Fell*	5 *Sty Head Pass*
3 *Yewbarrow*	6 *Lingmell*

L
4m
2h
**
ooo

Rabbit How and Eskdale Green. This makes a full day, but it is one of exceptional interest even without a visit to the castle. Another short version is to start the walk at Muncaster, cross the fell and return by train either from Irton Road or Eskdale Green stations.

Muncaster Castle, seat of the Penningtons since the thirteenth century, is famous for its Terrace Walk above the landscaped gardens where a collection of rhododendrons and azaleas and other ornamental shrubs thrive in the milder climate of south-west Cumbria. There are also wallabies, Himalayan bears and flamingoes on display as well as a collection of tropical birds. Indoors there are fine pieces of furniture, porcelains and tapestries to see. The old corn mill at Muncaster has been renovated by the Eskdale (Cumbria) Trust and is in working order producing wholemeal flour.

One of the curiosities of Muncaster Castle is an ancient green glass bowl enamelled in white and gilt. The bowl is one of several found throughout Lakeland which are known as 'lucks'. No one seems to know where the tradition came from, but many lucks are supposed to be gifts from the fairies. All bring luck to their owners and as a result are carefully preserved. The Muncaster luck is said to be the gift of Henry VI who was lost on Muncaster Fell after fleeing from the battle of Hexham in 1464. He was given shelter in the pele tower, which later became the grander castle of today, and he gave the bowl as a thanks offering. The luck which this particular bowl brings is that the castle would never lack a male heir.

The Romans built their sea port of Glannaventa just outside modern Ravenglass where the Esk and Mite reach the sea. Little remains of the Roman town apart from an exceptionally well preserved building which was part of the bath house. In Roman times supplies would come ashore here and be safe from attacks from the north beyond the Solway shores. They would then be carried up into the interior of what was then a military region, over Hard Knott and on to Carlisle and Hadrian's Wall. In those days Ravenglass would have been a much busier place than it is today.

Ravenglass is a breezy little town set between sand dunes and sea on one side

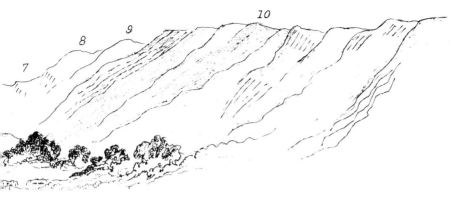

7   Great End
8   Scafell Pikes
9   Scafell

10   Illgill Screes

and Muncaster Fell on the other. Although its population is less than found
in many villages, it can claim the title
of a town having had a charter for a
market since 1209. A sandbar prevents
access by anything other than small
craft, but sea birds in their thousands nest
on a nearby bird sanctuary. Arrangements can be made with local boatmen to
ferry small parties across to the sanctuary. Tradition claims that the famous
Herwick sheep of Lakeland first came
ashore here from the wreck of a Spanish
galleon, but more likely they are of earlier
introduction by Norse settlers. Ravenglass's main attraction of course is that
the Ravenglass and Eskdale Railway
starts here by the side of the mainline
British Rail Station.

Next in the line of valleys dissecting the
Lakeland Fells is Wasdale. The strange
thing is that where often the valley takes
its name from its main river, in this case
there is no River Wast, but the name
comes from its famous lake — Wast
Water. Lingmell Beck flows in at one end
to mingle with the waters of Mosedale
and Nether Becks and they flow from
Wast Water as the River Irt. Perhaps the

valley should be Irt Dale, but Wasdale
sounds so much in keeping with this
mountainous region.

In its lower reaches the Irt flows
through gentle farm pasture from Santon
Bridge, but upstream from here the
scenery makes a rapid change through
low hills then steeply to the 1,900 ft-sides
of Wasdale. Santon Bridge is a small
cluster of houses with a campsite and an
hospitable pub that both cater for the
traveller. Again it is a good low level
centre when the weather is unkind higher
up. A walk upstream alongside the river
goes by way of Seedhill and Gatesgarth
farms to Hollins Bridge. Cross the river
here along the lane to Wrighthow Crags
and bear right to Stangends. Walk
through Great Coppice wood and cross
the road, then on to the path beneath
Latterbarrow, Shepherd Crags and Irton
Pike and back to Santon Bridge. The
walk has quite a few ups and downs, but
nowhere does it climb much more than
250 ft above the starting point, and that is
only 86 ft above sea level!

L
4½ m
2h
*
oo

Nether Wasdale, like Santon Bridge,
caters for the needs of the tourist with an
inn and a good campsite. Several short

L
3m
1½h
*
ooo

paths radiate from the village and many variations can be formed by linking one to the other. There is an interesting approach to the lake which starts at the southside of Forrest Bridge from the village. The way follows a farm track to Easthwaite, then crosses the Irt at Lund Bridge to join a path skirting the shore beneath Low Wood, where there is a magnificent view along the length of Wastwater to the high fells at its northern end. Continue along the lake side to the Youth hostel at Wasdale Hall and take the path by a cattle grid on the far side of the wood opposite the hall. This leads back to Nether Wasdale across Ashness How. There is a nature trail laid out in the grounds of Wasdale Hall which is open to anyone. A leaflet on sale at the hostel explains all the details.

Wast Water is 258 ft deep and is England's deepest lake with its bed 58 ft below sea level. Recently it was at the centre of a controversial plan to deepen the lake and use the water for the nearby nuclear power station. The plan has been shelved in favour of a scheme to take more from Ennerdale Water, but it highlights the vulnerability of our national heritage in the face of ever increasing demands to maintain our too readily accepted standards of living.

Looking up the length of Wast Water, on the right the mountain which rises steeply from the lake is Illgill Head. There is a footpath along the lake shore at the foot of the screes and even though for most of its length it is an easy scramble there is a particularly dangerous section of a quarter of a mile of awkward boulders. This particular section is beneath Bell Crag and the very aptly named Broken Rib. It is not a pleasant place and certainly not for anyone wearing less than stout walking boots.

L
5m
2½
***
oo

Wastwater

The Mountain Goat bus at Wasdale Head Inn

H
8 m
4½ h
***
ooo

A much more sensible way of becoming acquainted with Illgill How is to climb it by way of the track which starts at Lund Bridge at the downstream end of the lake. The path goes up the face of Whin Rigg alongside Greathall Gill and then joins another path coming on the right from Irton Fell to climb above the screes across the summit of Illgill Head before dropping down to Brackenclose Wood and the top end of Wastwater. There is a road walk back, but the views make it worth while. The Mountain Goat Bus Company have a service route up to Wasdale Head and this or a car driven by a non walking member of your party will be a useful means of returning to Lund Bridge, or wherever you started earlier.

Wasdale Head village has been a climbing centre for well over a century now and the Wastwater Hotel has accommodated many famous mountaineers in its day. Originally the village provided a resting place for packmen and sheep drovers travelling the early commercial trails through the mountains. The tiny church of St Olaf has been here for centuries and the general huddle of drystone buildings suggest that Wasdale Head was transported from some Alpine village long, long ago.

The highest summits of England surround Wasdale, but there is never the feeling of being shut in. The valley bottom is just wide enough and the peaks far enough back to give space to stand back and admire the majesty of the setting. Scafell Pike has a compelling fascination to all of us, for here is England's highest point, but it is a long hard slog to get up it. Of all those who stand on the summit cairn, by far the greatest number will have come the long hard grind from Langdale by way of the horrors of Rossett Gill; then there will be those who have laboured the shortest but steepest track from Wasdale by way of Brackenclose, while others will have come the more pleasant way from Borrowdale to Sty Head and Esk Hause. The smallest number who climb Scafell however will do so by the old guides' route or Corridor Route as it is known today. This is the oldest, and by far the most interesting way, up to the top of England. The Corridor Route was first developed in Victorian times when mountain tourists felt safer with a guide, and it links a series of grassy terraces across a very rough and wild mountain flank. It is an exciting, but safe route, and at the same time gains altitude with the least effort.

H
10m
6h
***
oooo

Starting from Wasdale Head climb the old pony track up Lingmell Beck to Sty Head. Follow the broad path to Esk Hause for a little way and then start to contour round to the right towards the head of Spouthead Gill. Gradually a well marked track appears and where this crosses the first gulley (Skew Gill) take the left-hand or upper track towards Greta Gill (the lower will lead you into difficulties). Go forward towards Lingmell Col but take your time and admire the wild scenery, especially into the depths of Piers Gill. At Lingmell Col either turn left and climb directly to the top by way of Dropping Crag or contour round through Hollow Stones to Mickledore and a left turn towards the last steep section and the summit cairn. The feeling of achievement as you stand on top of England cannot be diminished even if you are surrounded by large numbers of tourists, as the chances are that they will not have come up by such an interesting route as you have done.

Descend Scafell Pike by way of Mickledore, Hollow Stones and Brown Tongue to Brackenclose, but first a word of warning. Do not attempt to climb Scafell from Mickledore, ie the lower neighbour to Scafell Pike. Broad Stand beyond Mickledore looks fairly easy from a distance, but is for rock climbers only. The best way to climb Scafell from Wasdale is by way of Lord's Rake above Brown Tongue. It is a rough climb and one to be undertaken on a fine day only, but it is well worth doing if you are well shod and experienced in hill walking. On the return descend to Foxes Tarn and join the track coming up from Eskdale by Cam Spout. This will miss out the dangers of Broad Stand.

H
8m
5h
**
ooo

Of all the high summits, Great Gable is the one which looks the best from Wasdale. Its huge bulk rears massively at the dale head and draws the eye ever upward. The easiest route up it is from Honister and will be dealt with in a later chapter, but there is one for the more adventurously inclined. This is by the South or Climbers' Traverse and involves some scrambling on what to a rock climber is easy rock, but to an experienced walker it can prove to be quite an exciting expedition.

H
7m
7h
**
ooo

From Wasdale climb up to Sty Head by way of the Lingmell Beck track. At Sty Head take the lower of the two tracks which climb the flank of Great Gable. This track gradually gains height across grassy ledges to a series of huge boulders which eventually lead to Kern Knotts and then across the first of Gable's scree shoots, Great Hell Gate ('gate' is a local word for 'way'). Beyond this gully is the climbers' crag of Great Napes where there are some of the original British rock climbs; climbs explored by stalwarts like the Abraham brothers who took some of the earliest mountain photographs. On Great Napes aim for Napes Needle and behind it is an airy but safe ledge across the base of the crag to the aptly named Cat Rock and the Sphinx Rock and into the second scree shoot, Little Hell Gate. An easy scramble up the side of Little Hell Gate, partly on the scree and partly on rock, leads directly to the base of Westmorland Crags and on to the summit. The beautifully sited cairn on top of Westmorland Crags was erected in 1876 by two brothers of that name and it marks one of the finest viewpoints in the district, it rightly features on countless photographs.

All the ways down to Wasdale from Great Gable are steep and the usual route is by way of Windy Gap and Aaron Slack to Sty Head, but the really experienced and tough hill walker might continue his walk from Gable Summit to Beck Head and up the steep east side of Kirk Fell. Then descend to Black Sail Pass and a left turn down Gathering Beck into Mosedale and back to Wasdale Head. This will be a long hard day — but what an achievement!

H
7m
6h
***
oooo

Pillar mountain can be climbed from Wasdale Head by Mosedale and Black Sail Pass where a left turn follows the ridge all the way to the top of Pillar. From the summit the way back is by Wind Gap and left into Mosedale.

H
6m
3h
**
ooo

The summits around the head of Wast Water are all steep sided and the climbs correspondingly difficult, but it should not deter anyone who wants to admire these fine peaks without using too much energy from visiting this cradle of British Mountaineering. It is possible to get the feel of the hills by walking as far as you wish up any of the streams filling Wast Water. Lingmell and Mosedale are comparatively flat and easy walks, but Nether Beck half way down the lake is steep immediately above the road. However, higher up the angle is easier and the scenery quite dramatic as the fell sides begin to crowd in beneath Middle Fell and Seatallan.

L
3½m
2h
*
ooo

If an away-from-it-all picnic site is required then Greendale Tarn above Buckbarrow cannot be beaten. The path follows Greendale Beck direct from the back road to Gosforth.

Traditions die hard in remote mountain regions. It is not long ago that cattle were driven through the smoke of Beltane fires at the beginning of May to rid them of the evil influences of winter. This old Celtic custom has its real meaning lost in the mists of time. Yet another old custom, now thankfully gone, was that no child would have its arms washed or its hair

Gosforth Viking Cross

and finger nails cut before it was six months old in case it became a thief.

Ghosts haunt this area. Ghosts such as the one of Bjorn the outlaw who was hanged near Sty Head. In fact in the thirteenth century Sprinkling Tarn which drains on to Sty Head was known as 'Prentibourntern' (or the tarn of 'branded Bjorn'). The whole wild area around Sty Head is described by Sir Hugh Walpole in *Rogue Herries*. Another ghost story tells of a corpse being taken by horseback over Burnmoor to Eskdale in the days before Wasdale Head had its own graveyard. On the bleak moor something startled the horse and it bolted and was lost never to be found. Locals say that on stormy days the wild horse with its macabre load can be seen galloping across the moors.

Viking settlers must have felt very much at home as they developed their farmsteads on the good grazing land found in the safe sheltered valleys. They raised the tall slender cross at Gosforth about four miles to the west of Wasdale; this 15 ft-high cross shows a combination of Christian and Nordic pagan designs all interwoven in delicate plaited carving. Gosforth has seen the centuries quietly pass by. There are three stone circles just outside the village and a series of nine small cairns connected with them. Its church has been in use through Viking and Anglo Saxon times and provides a link through the nearby seventeenth-century houses right up to the present day.

In complete contrast to these ancient stones, the twentieth century is reached at the nearby Windscale and Calder Works of British Nuclear Fuels. The public are permitted into the complex of modern technology and anyone wishing to visit should first telephone Seascale 333. Calder Hall is a nuclear power station providing electricity for our ever increasing fuel demands. Despite being surrounded by controversy, nuclear power must surely become one of our major sources of energy as fossilised fuels are gradually used up. At the Windscale Works irradiated fuel from both British and foreign nuclear reactors is reprocessed and plutonium and unused uranium are extracted for future use.

5 Ennerdale to Buttermere

The narrow coastal plain to the west of the lakes and peaks contains most of Cumbria's industry. This industry is based on coal, chemicals and access to the sea, but most visitors to the Lake District usually dismiss this section of the coast as uninteresting and unworthy of inspection. While agreeing that an industrial site, either old or modern, is hardly in the category of a holiday experience, the coastal area has interest waiting for the visitor prepared to seek it out.

Inland the valleys radiate outward from the central pivot of Great Gable. Valleys deep and remote as the Calder and Ennerdale can only be explored on foot, but there is also the Cocker Valley which in its upper reaches is flooded with the twin lakes of Buttermere and Crummock Water. The motorised tourist is fortunate in that a motor road follows the length of the Cocker Valley all the way from Honister Hause to Cockermouth.

The western lakes provide excellent sport for the angler, especially the angler prepared to walk a few miles from his car to where the best fish are hiding. Between the valleys high independant peaks rise up south of Ennerdale and to the north airy ridges mark the complex of watersheds. All this area makes for exciting high level mountain walking.

As the previous chapter ended by the coast it is logical to follow northwards through the coastal towns before turning into the valleys and ridges. At Egremont there has been a market since 1267, while its ancient castle was built by the Normans on the site of an earlier fortification. Here the inhabitants were besieged by Robert the Bruce and later by Lord James Douglas in the many border wars of earlier times. One of its heirs the 'boy of Egremont' was destined to become King of Scotland, but he was drowned in a boating accident in the Solway. The tragedy is recorded in many ballads written at the time and they tell of the endless sorrow that his family felt at their loss. The legend of the Horn of Egremont says that it can only be made to sound by the rightful lord of the castle.

The pink cliffs of St Bees Head are the most westerly part of Lakeland and their 300 ft shelter a pleasant sandy bathing beach below the pretty resort of St Bees. It was at this spot that the Irish nun St Bega was shipwrecked in the seventh century. Along with a few surviving followers she was befriended by Lady Egremont and given shelter at the castle. The saint and the lady of the castle became firm friends and when the nuns wished to build a sanctuary Lady Egremont pursuaded her husband to give them land and materials. He agreed to give the stone and timber, but only offered that land which would be covered by snow the following morning. As it was then midsummer, the nuns thought their request was to be denied. Tradition states that when the next morning dawned part of the land between the castle and the sea was covered by snow. Lord Egremont realised that this was the work of someone more powerful than himself and readily gave that land to the nuns.

A less romantic legend at nearby Rottington tells that the bones of a Viking giant — Rottin — were buried there. Rottin and his shipmates carried off several nuns from the abbey and kept them as slaves until one of their number managed to drug their captors and escaped after stabbing the Vikings to death.

Gatehouse, Egremont Castle

The industrial part of Whitehaven became a boom town in the seventeenth century with the discovery of coal along the coast. Although it is far from the centre of mainland activity, Whitehaven has had its moments of excitement. John Paul Jones the American privateer sailed into the harbour with his ship the *Ranger*, but the solid citizens of Whitehaven resisted his efforts and he left in something of a hurry. In 1915 a marauding German submarine surfaced opposite the town and bombarded the place for a time. Details of this incident and others can be found in the museum of coal mining and local industry in the Market Place. Steel making and salmon fishing are two of the widely diverse industries of Workington where coal is mined far out under the Irish Sea. Mary Queen of Scots was landed here as a captive and wrote a letter of appeal to Queen Elizabeth from Workington Hall, but as we know, this was to no avail.

Discoveries of Roman remains at Maryport have recently led to the theory that Hadrian's Wall continued right round the Cumberland coast from the Solway. If this is true, and certainly there are military reasons for guarding the shore of this impenetrable mountain region, then the logistics of garrisoning such a huge and complex fortification stretching right away across to the mouth of the Tyne would have been formidable. Ports such as Ravenglass, Whitehaven and Maryport would have been hives of activity with the import of men and materials and the export of metal and hides.

The oldest and most interesting part of the town is by the quay. The town as we see it today was laid out in the middle of the eighteenth century by Humphrey Stenhouse, Lord of the manor. Until then the village was known as Ellenfoot, but he changed the name to Maryport after his wife's name when he decided to develop the place as a coal port. A town trail guides the visitor around the old part of the town. Details of this can be found in the small booklet on sale at the tourist and information centre, which is attached to the small museum devoted to the vessels which have sailed in and out of this west Cumberland port.

The Romans built Derventio just north of here to command the major routes north west of the Lakeland hills. Later a castle was built above the River Derwent at its confluence with the Cocker. Little remains of the original building erected by William de Fortibus, who used the natural defences offered by the two rivers to foil attack by Scottish raiders in the mid-thirteenth century. Most of what we see today is the result of later additions up to the beginning of the eighteenth century. Some of the stones from Roman Derventio were used to build the castle. The most important is an altar which was found on the north side of the gatehouse. Mary Queen of Scots was lodged for a night here in 1568, and some indication of the hardships she endured while a prisoner on the move can be got from a touching incident which occured while she was imprisoned in the castle. After her defeat at Langside she was brought here via the port of Workington with nothing other than the travel-stained clothes she stood in. Sir Henry Fletcher noticing how dirty her clothing was, presented her with several yards of crimson velvet. This act of kindness was later acknowledged by her son when he became King James of England.

The busy market town of modern Cockermouth is a regular meeting place for West Cumbrian farmers. Six roads, all from farming country, meet here and Monday is the day when the fat sheep and cattle are brought in for sale. Frenzied activity builds up early around the auctioneer's stand and if you do not get in the way you will enjoy an entertaining hour or so listening to the bidding, often in the old Cumbrian dialect. As Cockermouth is at the junction of so many roads

PLACES TO VISIT IN THE WHITEHAVEN AREA:

Egremont Castle
An early Norman site with the ruins of the twelfth-century castle in a public park.

Whitehaven Museum, Market Place, Whitehaven
Upper floor has exhibits on geology, archaeology, industrial history and maritime history of the area. Travelling and special exhibitions on ground floor.

Maryport Maritime Museum, Senhouse Street, Maryport
A small museum with displays relating to the port and its vessels.

Helena Thompson Museum, Park End Road, Workington
Exhibition of mainly Victorian objects, costumes, furniture, silver, ceramics, glass, pictures and prints.

from hill country it is an ideal centre for exploring the western fells and valleys. The Trout Hotel in the main street has long been popular amongst anglers; Bing Crosby was a regular visitor who came to enjoy its quiet hospitality on his fishing trips to Britain.

A pleasant riverside ramble starts at Papcastle across the river from Cockermouth. It follows the north bank downstream as far as the third feeder stream joining from the right. Turn right here and follow it to the second road bridge and then right again uphill for just under a quarter of a mile. Another right turn across fields leads to Papcastle. The last section of the walk is along the line of a Roman road to the fort of Derventio on the outskirts of Papcastle. Regretably much of the fort is now obliterated by modern development.

L
5m
2½h
**
ooo

Leaving the towns and industry of Western Cumberland for the lakes and hills the A5086 skirts the foot of the outlying moorland on its way past sleepy villages towards Egremont and the coast. John Dalton the father of modern chemistry came from Eaglesfield, a village two miles south west of Cockermouth and Fletcher Christian of the 'Mutiny on the Bounty' fame, was born at Moorland Close just outside the village.

Traces of iron ore mining which led to the development of the Cumbrian steel industry can be found on either side of the A5086. The mines are usually marked by the spoil heaps and outcrops of red shale are a sure indication of iron rich rock. The old mineral railway which served the mines has also gone, but again it can be traced by ruined cuttings and bridges.

The high and almost trackless moorland marking the south-western boundary of the Lakeland peaks reaches up in a deeply indented escarpment ending abruptly in the steep crags of Pillar and Haycock mountains. It is a mysterious place once frequented by our early ancestors who left their memorials in the form of the complex of cairns and stone circles on Stockdale Moor. Few people except shepherds come this way in the twentieth century, but once when the climate was milder than it is now the land supported a large agrarian economy. To-day the land is only suitable for sheep rearing and forestry.

The valleys now partly flooded by Ennerdale Water, Buttermere, and Crummock Water were created by massive glacial action moving outwards from a central point. At a later date smaller glaciers filled the high and usually north facing combes and this in turn led to the creation of the steep crags on the north sides of the ridges which divide the valleys from each other.

Buttermere, Crummock Water and Loweswater are easily accessible by road, but Cogra Moss and Ennerdale Water are for pedestrians only. Roads go to within a short distance of them, but to get the best value out of a visit to either it is necessary to leave the car and walk.

To reach Ennerdale, the most dramatic of all Lakeland valleys, means a long drive unless you stay at one of the very few places offering accommodation at this side of the Lakes. Even if it is a long drive the valley is worth the effort. Cars must be left at Bowness Knott car park as the road beyond is closed to all except authorised traffic.

On leaving the car, the pedestrian possibilities soon become obvious. A gentle saunter round the Smithy Beck nature trail from the car park (leaflets describing the trail are available nearby), may be all that is needed to occupy a very pleasant and interesting afternoon. Or alternatively the Nine Becks walk, mainly through the forest on the south side of Ennerdale, is more adventurous. Both walks are safe in all but the most arctic weather as they are waymarked by a system of colour coded stakes. Check the details of this on the large scale diagram by the car park. An easily followed footpath goes right round the lake. All that is necessary is that you keep the lake-shore on your right if walking in a clockwise direction, or left if anticlockwise. The only time that the lake is abandoned is in the crossing of the river Liza at a point about halfway between the lake and Ennerdale Youth Hostel.

L
2/3
1h
*
ooo

M
9m
4h
*
ooo

L
7m
3½
**
ooo

Ennerdale Water has long been a popular fishing lake for the devoted angler. Anglers Crag above its southern shore denotes this interest and the river where it flows into the lake is known as Char Dub, or Char Pool. It is necessary to take out a licence from the North West Water Authority to fish in any water having a surface area of more than 1 hectare (2·4 acres). Some waters are owned or let to clubs and it will probably be necessary to buy a permit locally but

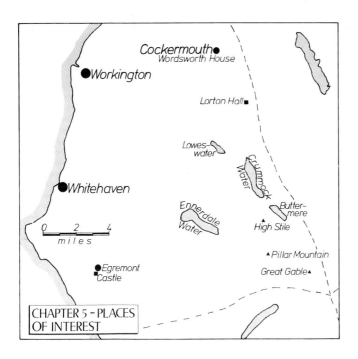

good fishing can be found here as in almost all the Lakeland lakes and rivers.

The ever increasing demands on water resources have made the planners look at Ennerdale as a source of supply. It is already supplying water to Whitehaven, but the growing needs of British Nuclear Fuels at its Windscale plant, together with the growth of industrial West Cumbria, have led to plans to take more water and no doubt increase the size of Ennerdale Water. Industrial links with Ennerdale are nothing new. At the western end of the lake a group of cottage buildings known as Bleachworks Cottages mark the use of water in the days when freshly woven fabric was bleached by frequent washing followed by open-air drying.

The river which feeds Ennerdale lake is the Liza. The name comes from an old Norse word 'lysa' which means 'bright water'. It is not difficult to imagine the early Viking settlers coming to this secluded valley and feeling very much at home. The steep sides rising from the lake are very similar to Norwegian fjord country. Careful examination of the field on the south side of Char Dub will show what are the foundations of Viking or Saxon homesteads. How old these are has not been decided, but it is easy to imagine that here was where the early Viking settlers to our country made their home.

The one word which aptly describes Ennerdale is solitude; there are two youth hostels, a climbing hut and a farm, nothing more. No supermarkets, bingo halls or pubs — just mountains, trees and solitude. To enter this valley the tourist must be independent and self reliant. No matter how crowded the other places are, at least the chances here are that you are on your own and will probably only meet a handful of people all day. It does not matter if you only walk from the car park as far as Black Sail hostel and back, or

View from above Buttermere Village

1 High Bank	5 Great Gable
2 Honister Crag	6 Hay Stacks
3 Green Crag	7 Kirk Fell & Scarf Gap (below)
4 Green Gable	8 High Crag

even climb Pillar mountain, you will feel you have the place almost to yourself, and other walkers, far from being intrusive, will pass as a welcome face along the track. Such is the freedom of the fells to those prepared to seek it.

The upper reaches of Ennerdale are bounded on both sides by a complex line of summits, starting with smooth sided fells and moorland above and to the west of the lake. To the south of Ennerdale Youth Hostel the rock has changed from slate to materials of volcanic origin and these have created the rugged masses of Haycock, Steeple and Pillar. Kirk Fell rears up its twin summits in graceful symmetry bounded on one side by Black Sail Pass and the other by Beck Head. Great Gable sits in majesty at the hub of ridges radiating west and north. The north side of the valley is edged above Black Sail youth hostel by the curious and aptly named multi-summits of Haystacks, before sweeping down to Scarth Gap and then climbing up to the exhilarating ridge of High Stile.

As the best routes along High Stile start and finish around Buttermere we can leave that treat in store for a few paragraphs and concentrate essentially on the hills south and east of the lake. So in dealing with the high ridges we start with Haycock and move around in an anticlockwise direction along the Pillar ridges to Great Gable and then on to Haystacks.

The massive dome of Haycock which marks the watershed between Wasdale and Ennerdale is often neglected by walkers in favour of the summits further east. It can be climbed for its own merit, or as the start of a long ridge walk over Scoat Fell and Pillar before descending left at Black Sail.

The best route up Haycock starts at Char Dub and climbs the steep but easy ridge between Deep Gill and Silverhow Beck to the depression between Caw Fell and Little Gowder Crag. Turn left here and follow the wall across the summit ridge to the top of Haycock. To return follow the wall eastwards (a safe route in mist) down to the col before the climb to Little Scoat Fell. Do not climb upwards but turn left and avoid Deep Gill by contouring round to Tewit How and then

H
5½ m
3h
* * *
ooo

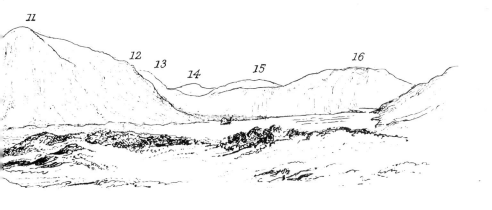

downhill steeply to Tongue End and the valley bottom. Tongue End is the vee shaped wedge of treeless moor below Lingmell and is a deliberately made funnel to guide sheep down into the valley at shearing and lambing time.

H
3½ m
2 h
★★★★
ooo

Scoat Fell can be included with Haycock in the return route across the imaginatively named Steeple to the north. The airy ridge is fine in summer and dry conditions, but like all narrow ridges should be treated with care in bad weather. The section of path below Long Crag is indistinct and care must be taken here. Either follow Low Beck or contour round to the drove way at Tongue End for safety.

The shepherds of old had the inspiration to name Pillar mountain. Its rugged mass dominates the upper reaches of Ennerdale and since the infancy of rock climbing has long been a magnet attracting climbers to test their skills on its northern flank. The name Pillar is in fact the name given to the huge bastion of rock halfway up the fell side between the forest and the actual summit. The summit is wide and flat and almost a dis-

appointment, but fortunately this is overcome by the awesome grandeur of its craggy north face. While the route described earlier across Great Gables' climbing face is about as far as even the best hillwalker should go in attempting to join rock climbers, the high level route up Pillar is safe and entertaining. The route starts at Black Sail Youth Hostel and climbs to Black Sail Pass by the old pony route. At the summit of the pass turn right and follow the remains of the boundary fence across Looking Stead. Above Green Cove the track divides. Take the one traversing right to the conspicuously sited Robinsons' Cairn, then across a boulder strewn hollow to the foot of Shamrock. Turn left and upwards on a scree slope to a wide rake, or ledge on the right. This is the Shamrock Traverse, follow it as far as the first aid box above Pisgah which marks the top of Pillar Rock. A left turn and a scramble up steep scree leads to the summit of Pillar. To return, turn left and follow the ridge back to Black Sail Pass. This is a magnificent walk through some of the most exciting rock scenery in Britain. Provid-

H
5 m
5 h
★★★★
oooo

Buttermere

ing the day and weather have been chosen with care and the path followed closely, especially on Shamrock Traverse, then it is a safe and enjoyable route.

Kirk Fell stands between Pillar and Gable. Which ever way we look at it, its sides are steep and there is no path which even tries to follow an easy route. They all go straight up! The best route is to turn left at Black Sail Pass and follow the boundary fence across the twin summits to Beck Head and back to Ennerdale via Stone Cove and the Tongue. Alternatively an interesting route traverses round above Boat How to the Black Sail track.

H
4m
4h
***
ooo

Great Gable has many routes, some have already been described in Chapter 4 and another again in Chapter 6. From Black Sail Hostel the direct way climbs the Tongue to Windy Gap, then turns right and goes very steeply up loose stones to the summit. This way is for masochists. There are far better routes on this mountain, but for some unknown reason it is, with variations in the approach, the one most favoured by the thousands who visit Gable annually. (See Chapter 6 for the most enjoyable route).

H
4½m
5h
***
oo

The fascinating mixture of tarns, crags, scree, rocks and moorland comprising Haystacks make this little mountain an absolute gem just waiting to be explored. It is not as high as its neighbours, but what it lacks in height is made up by variety. Any visitor to either Ennerdale or nearby Buttermere who has only a day to spare and wants to climb, then this is the one for them. It is an entertaining mountain. Even the summit is unique for one of its many beautiful tarns, some even dotted with islands, can be found almost on top of the mountain.

H
3½m
3½h
***
oooo

To climb Haystacks from Ennerdale walk up the side of Loft Beck beyond Black Sail Hostel. At the ruins of a boundary fence, either turn left and cross the line of the seven stacks to the top, or alternatively aim across from the fence to Blackbeck Tarn and follow the path passing Innominate Tarn and on to the summit. This is a hill to explore all day, so do not keep to any recognised route unless the weather is bad. Wander amongst the crags and perhaps picnic by one of the tarns. A return route can be found by way of the western flank as far as Scarth Gap and a left turn downhill into the valley below the hostel.

The Buttermere valley and Ennerdale are only two miles apart at their narrowest, but where Ennerdale is solitude, Buttermere is bustle and traffic. Fortunately it rarely gets overcrowded and thereby holds its charm.

Just by the junction of the Loweswater road and the A5086 is Mockerlin Tarn. Although almost insignificant compared with the larger lakes, it is full of interest to anyone prepared to question the reason of nature. When the glaciers were retreating,

Splitting stone at Honister Quarry

occasionally a large block of ice was slow to melt and became embedded in silt and debris. When this block eventually melted it formed a steep sided lake known as a kettlehole. This is now Mockerlin Tarn. Another interesting feature is that this tarn, along with other still water tarns, is slowly filling with vegetation and peat and will one day become a bog.

M
5½m
3h
**
ooo

Beyond Mockerlin village is quiet Loweswater. The road passes along its northern shore and there is a circular walk which starts a little further on towards the village of Loweswater. Take the lane below High Cross and drop down to Dub Beck. Keep right and walk along the track to Watergate Farm and the lakeside into Holme Wood. Follow this as far as Hudson Place then take the track behind the farm across the fields to Jenkinson Place. Bear left at Iredale Place and climb gently up the hillside to a junction with another track. Turn sharp left here and contour round the flanks of Burnbank Fell and Carling Knott above Holme Wood to Highnook Beck. Turn left and cross to the other side of the valley and follow the straight path to High Nook Farm and back to the road.

Fox hunting is an energetic sport, but nowhere more so than in the Lake District. Here they hunt on foot with packs of tough hounds. Of the many packs the Mellbreak can claim to have had the champion huntsman as one of its members. Jonathan Banks of Loweswater accounted for 1,800 foxes up until his death in January 1928.

One thing about the Lakes is the ability it offers to get away from ones fellow men whenever the need arises. Mosedale is one such place. Even if the Buttermere road is busy the peace offered by Mosedale to the pedestrian will quickly balance things. Start by the Kirkstile Inn at Loweswater and follow the grassy lane across Park Beck and through the narrow portals into Mosedale. After about 1¼ miles of walking the track divides, so take

L
6m
3h
**
oooo

the one which climbs left across the side of Mellbreak until it meets with a path coming from Ennerdale. Turn left and follow Black Beck down to Crummock Water but on the way down cross over and take a look at the 120ft falls of Scale Force opposite. Follow the shore line of Crummock Water until the lake starts to narrow and then leave it to walk across fields to Muncaster House where a left turn leads back to Loweswater.

The direct ascent of Mellbreak from Loweswater is made by following the Mosedale path as far as the gate beyond the ancient earthwork. Through the gate turn left and climb slanting left to a steep ridge which leads directly to the top of Mellbreak. Return by walking towards the southern summit as far as a slight col and turn right. A path gradually appears slanting downhill into Mosedale.

H
4m
3h
***
ooo

At one time the roads from Keswick to the Buttermere valley struck terror into the hearts of motorists, but now it is only the 'old banger' pulling a caravan which creates problems for the AA and RAC patrols. The circular drive along Borrowdale and over Honister Pass to Buttermere and back over Newlands or Whinlatter are drives of pure delight. Pause where the Honister road cuts through wild and lonely fells before dropping down to the smiling face of Buttermere.

Crummock Water and Buttermere Lake were once a single lake which was divided by debris deposited by streams rapidly erroding the unstabilised hillsides immediately after the last ice age. The old Fish Inn at Buttermere stands by Mill Beck which created this alluvial delta which now provides some of the best grazing in the valley.

A short easy walk from Buttermere car park across flowery meadows to Crummock Water and on to Black Beck leads upwards to Scale Force. This fall between sheer rock walls is the loftiest in Lakeland and should be a 'must' for visitors to the

L
4m
1½h
**
oooo

Honister Pass

View from Lanthwaite Wood, below Crummock Water

1 Grasmoor
2 Honister Crag
3 Green Gable
4 Great End
5 Great Gable
6 Hay Stacks
7 Scafell
8 Kirk Fell
9 High Crag
10 High Stile
11 Bleaberry Tarn
12 Red Pike

H
7m
5h
★★★★
oooo

area. Another fall nearby is Sourmilk Gill. It marks the route to one of the finest ridge walks in the area, a walk which starts from the exit stream from Buttermere and climbs up through Burtness Woods to Bleaberry Tarn. After resting by the tarn turn right and climb the ridge on to Red Pike then left along Chapel Crags to High Stile, High Crag and down to Scarth Gap. Turn left at the pass and follow the path down to Buttermere Lake, following the south bank back to Burtness Woods and the village.

If you are lucky enough to be on Red Pike in spring or autumn on a day when the valleys are full of mist, but the ridges are in clear sunshine, perhaps you will be fortunate enough to experience the 'brocken spectre' effect. This is when a low westerly sun, ie in spring or autumn, is behind the climber standing above a mist filled combe. A huge shadow topped by a halo is formed and the whole effect is rather weird to say the least. This phenomena can be found on any mountain with a north or east facing combe such as Red Pike or Coniston Old Man.

Haystacks can be climbed from Buttermere by way of Scarth Gap and returning down Warnscale Beck or even on to Fleetwith over Honister Crag, but this involves some very steep downhill walking which can be dangerous in wet weather. Note the memorial cross beneath Low Raven Crag!

The range of fells above Buttermere and Crummock Water can be climbed from this side, but it is easier from Bassenthwaite as this is less steep and the access valleys are longer. However having said that we cannot lightly dismiss either the walking or the scenery and buildings on the northern side of the valley. There are ancient tracks crossing over the fells by high cols. The one from Sail Beck to Stair preceded the Newlands road by centuries and the path which climbs Gasgale Gill from Lanthwaite at the far end of Crummock was a quick way over to Braithwaite and Keswick market for the farm folk living around Loweswater and Crummock Water.

Steep hills on either side of the Newlands Pass above Buttermere must bring

H
4m
3h
★★★
oooo

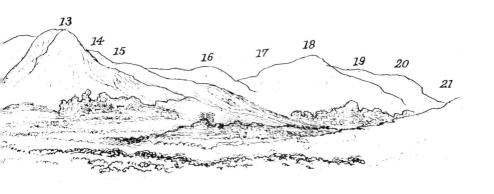

13	Mellbreak	19	Loweswater (below)
14	Hen Comb	20	Burnbank Fell
15	Gavel Fell	21	Road to Ennerdale & Wastwater
16	Middle Fell		
17	Blake Fell		
18	Carling Knott		

Buttermere

Buttermere Village

H
5½m
4h+
****
oooo

this chapter to a close, but of course the almost perfect pyramid of Whiteless Pike cannot be ignored. The popular track which starts behind Buttermere Post Office is not as steep as a first glance might suggest. It climbs zig-zagging on the steepest parts directly to the top of Whiteless. Beyond the summit a track continues across the fine high level route over Wandope, Crag Hill and Stile End to Braithwaite. Return to Buttermere on the Mountain Goat Mini Bus unless you wish to make other arrangements.

6 Bassenthwaite to Borrowdale

The north-west corner of the Lake District is divided into two sharply contrasting halves by the bulky masses of Skiddaw and Blencathra. To the north the hills, with one exception, have smooth rounded slopes and few ridges; they are almost devoid of surface stone and on first glance do not appear to offer the same excitement as their sisters across the Derwent valley. This is country best known to shepherds and those fell-walkers who are adventurous enough to explore off the beaten track.

Altering the pattern set by earlier chapters we will start with the most northerly part of this district and move to its middle and more popular regions in an anticlockwise direction.

The people of northern Cumbria have always shown an independence of character, with none more so than John Peel the famed huntsman who came from Caldbeck. Throughout his long life he enjoyed the exhilaration of fox hunting with his hounds over these remote fells; he was immortalised by the ballad *D'ye ken John Peel* which was written by his friend John Woodcock Graves in 1832. Although Peel spent most of his life about six miles away at Ruthwaite, when he died he was buried at Caldbeck.

Men of Caldbeck have mined the fells south of the village since the sixteenth century. At least ten major mines were worked and one, Roughton Gill, now worked out, is said to have yielded twenty-three different ores and other minerals. Today only two mines, Sandbed and Potts Gill are operative and are producing barytes (barium sulphate) for use in the glass and paint industries. Tunnels and shafts penetrate for a great way beneath the hillside and as most are in a dangerous condition any exploration should be restricted to viewing the entrances from a safe distance. Remember that this is a remote district and it is likely that no one would be around to help if a latter-day prospector got into difficulties on a trip below ground.

A mass of hills separated from Skiddaw forest by the River Caldew come under the generic titles of the Caldbeck and Uldale Fells and can easily be explored from a car parked along the back lanes at their feet.

From Mosedale, Carrock Fell can be climbed by a little used path which starts from the mine track a little way above the River Caldew. The track zig zags its way to the summit through an area of rocks and scree which are a geologist's paradise. Carrock Fell is the odd one out in the northern fells and the reason is that it is composed of igneous and volcanic rocks which have been thrust up through the shales of the hills north of Skiddaw. There is even an outcrop of gabbro, a rough rock also found in the Cuillin of Skye. This is a mountain of many interests, the summit is crowned with a circle of stones which are the remains of an ancient fortification and lower down is Carrock mine which produced the heavy metal tungsten, until a fall in world prices made the mine uneconomical. | H
3m
2h
***
ooo |

From Nether Row a mile or so to the south of Caldbeck the mine road to Potts Gill mine can be used as a starting point to explore the ruins of old mining activity (from the surface only), and then on to High Pike. A strong party could continue round to Carrock Fell, but unless transport can be arranged to meet them at Mosedale there is a long walk back along the mine road. | H
4½m
3h
**
ooo |

So few walkers use these fells that the heather moors have become a haven for wild life not readily seen on the central peaks. Anyone finding the central areas too crowded, say on a Bank Holiday weekend will be well advised to motor round to Longlands beyond Bassenthwaite village and turn their attention to the Uldale Fells. The delightful advantage of these fells is that they are within easy reach of Keswick or Cockermouth by road and yet are comparatively unknown.

Uldale Fells have Knott as their pivot. Four grassy ridges which in turn divide in their lower reaches, radiate outwards like the spokes of a wheel. They are all good and easy to walk over either in short or long tours, although they require carefully planned return transport.

H
6m
4h
****
oo

As several days can be spent exploring these fells, perhaps the best assistance this guide can offer is to describe a central route which can be shortened or lengthened at will to include as many tops and ridges as are desired. The only thing to bear in mind is the fact that as these are not well trodden fells, tracks are few and far between and therefore route finding is not easy in mist and rain. From the old road between Longlands and Greenhead take the bridle track which starts a little way beyond an old sandpit. Turn right and climb easily along the grassy road above Carleton Gill as far as Great Sca Fell where the track peters out. Turn half right on Great Sca Fell and cross a boggy col to climb steadily to the summit of Knott. The return route can be made by following Frozenfell Gill down until the deep cutting of Trusmadoor is seen on the right. Pass through the 'door' on a gradually improving path which crosses the river Ellen on its way down to Longlands.

All the tops above Longlands can be visited by using either of the paths just mentioned or the day can be extended beyond Knott by crossing Coombe Height and dropping down to Mosedale by the side of the river Caldew. Transport must be arranged from Mosedale otherwise it will be a long walk back home again!

H
7m
5h
****
oo

Skiddaw, that heavy old benevolent giant, can claim to have seen all the events which led to the formation of the scenery of Lakeland. Its rocks are far older than those of volcanic origin which make up the central, and only slightly higher, peaks. Its name comes from the old Norse for 'craggy hill', an apt description of its stoney flanks. As it is an easy mountain to climb, Skiddaw is ascended by thousands every year, but that does not detract from its beauty. The views all around, and especially over Derwentwater, are breathtaking and make the effort of the slog from Keswick more than worthwhile.

The people of Keswick and surrounding villages have long held a special affection for this mountain which makes a perfect backcloth to countless views. Once they used to light beacon fires on the summit in time of trouble, but now visitors to its airy heights do so for peaceful reasons. The wide path up from Keswick was the first one to be created up a Lakeland mountain top over a century ago. Skiddaw was home for George Smith who came from Banffshire in 1864. George was a Victorian recluse who decided to make himself a hermitage in a sort of nest perched on a ledge on Skiddaw Dodd, which could only be entered by climbing into a small cave. He was a good painter of portraits and he usually traded these for whisky. This however, was his undoing for he became an alcoholic and was constantly in trouble with the police.

Most of the visitors to Skiddaw do so by climbing the Keswick path, but there are other ways and all of them more interesting. The inhabitants of Bassenthwaite will tell you that theirs is the best route to Skiddaw. Certainly they enjoy

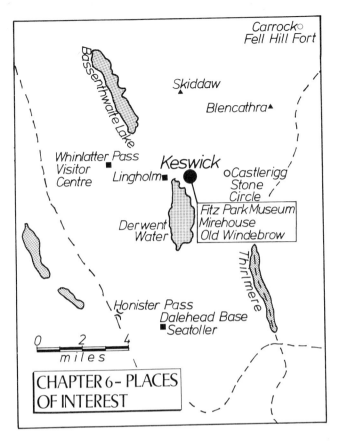

CHAPTER 6 – PLACES
OF INTEREST

the magnificent sunset glows reflected from the western flanks of the mountain. The route from Bassenthwaite goes through Barkbeth Farm and follows Southerndale Beck to Carlside col where a left turn leads up a scree slope to the summit ridge of Skiddaw.

H
8½m
5h
***
ooo

The straight lines formed in the screes at the head of Southerndale are not man-made but are formed by alternate thawing and freezing. The technical term for this is 'solifluction'.

As there is a regular bus service between Keswick and Bassenthwaite any ascent of Skiddaw can be made more interesting by descending to either place and using the bus back to base. Also the tour of Skiddaw can be done this way. The best approach is to take the bus to

where the minor road forks from the A591 at High Side. Follow this narrow road for 1½ miles as far as Peter House Farm. Turn right immediately before the farm buildings along a rough road which climbs up the side of Dash Beck valley. Pass the series of plunges that go to make Whitewater Dash waterfall and continue over the watershed to the row of shepherd's cottages known as Skiddaw House. Climb by the footpath around the end of Burnt Horse ridge and across the final watershed into the upper reaches of the valley of Glenderaterra Beck. A delightful path following the 1,200 ft contour skirts round the flank of Lonscale Fell to join the Skiddaw path down to Keswick.

M
10m
5h
**
ooo

Before leaving Skiddaw, mention must be made of two other grand alternatives

View from Latrigg on the way to Skiddaw
(Note that Keswick is now much larger than depicted here.)

1	*Walla Crag*	8	*Great End*
2	*Falcon Crag*	9	*Scafell Pike*
3	*Brown Knotts*	10	*Scafell, Gatecrag (below)*
4	*Castlehead (below)*	11	*Blea Crag*
5	*Glaramara, Brund (below)*	12	*Maiden Moor*
6	*Hanging Knot*	13	*Catbells*
7	*Castle Crag (below)*	14	*Hindscarth*

H
6m
3½h
****
ooo

to the normal route. The first starts at the Ravenstone Hotel on the A591 by climbing steeply to the 600 ft contour along a fire break. It then slants upward to join The Edge where a right turn leads upward across Ullock Pike, Long Side and down to Carlside col before climbing the last bit on to Skiddaw across the boulder field of Broad End. In dry weather this is an easy and safe climb mostly along a narrow turf ridge.

H
5m
3½h
***
ooo

The final alternative starts at Millbeck village and climbs either directly alongside Mill Beck or over Whitestones and Carlside to Carlside Col to join the rough way up to the south top and the start of Skiddaw's summit ridge.

The unspoilt quiet villages of Uldale, Ruthwaite, the Irebys and Bassenthwaite lie at the foot of the western fells, and all are bypassed by the main roads. Gentle country leads to the Solway plain on one side and high hills the other. Uncrowded caravan sites and campsites are here in quiet seclusion.

Bassenthwaite lake is better known to the fishing fraternity than by the general tourist. Somehow with its close proximity to Derwentwater it often gets overlooked. The busy A66 hugs its western shore, but the eastern shore is perfection indeed with a quiet charm of flowery meadows and woodlands. A little used path follows the eastern bank from the main road at Mire House near Little Crosthwaite. Sometimes it wanders inland a little to avoid private property, but soon it returns to the shoreline which can be followed all the way to the luxury hotel which now occupies the Victorian mansion of Armathwaite Hall. A short walk to the A591 and a bus ride back to Keswick completes the delightful circle.

L
4m
2h
**
ooo

The fells above the western shore of Bassenthwaite are steep sided and densely forested and as a result are not easy to climb. With one exception the Grizedale and Hopegill Fells beyond Whinlatter are much more interesting. This exception is Barf which is climbed by following a forest track to the side of Beckstones Gill above the Swan Hotel. From Barf the walk can be continued to Lords Seat and down through the forest to the top of

H
3m
2½h
***
oo

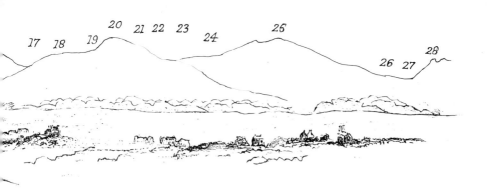

the Whinlatter Pass to catch a Mountain Goat minibus to Braithwaite and the Cumberland Motor Services bus to the Swan Hotel.

The Forestry Commission have opened a useful visitor centre at the top of Whinlatter and have produced an excellently illustrated booklet under the title of 'Thornthwaite' which deals with the forests of either side of Whinlatter Pass. The Commission have also laid out a number of short walks from the car park at Noble Knott above Braithwaite.

Visitors to the Swan Hotel will be intrigued by the conspicuous white rock towering above a steep scree slope beyond the field on the opposite side of the road from the hotel. This is the 'Bishop' in his pulpit. Anyone with strong lungs and legs can visit him by scrambling up the steep scree, almost slipping back two steps for every one forward. Close inspection will reveal that the Bishop is a whitewashed rock precariously separated from the main fell by a narrow shelf. The publican from the Swan is traditionally responsible for his

raiment and local volunteers annually carry buckets of whitewash up the slope to repaint this unique landmark. In the small meadow at the foot of the Bishop is another lesser known rock, often hard to find when the grass is high. This is the 'Clerk' who sits patiently listening to the interminable sermon from above.

The valleys of Coledale and Newlands to the west and south of Braithwaite cut deeply into some of the best fell walkers' hills. The whole continuous line from Grisedale Pike across the Newlands Pass to Robinson and Dale Head, then north over Maiden Moor to Cat Bells will evoke happy memories in the minds of those who tread their rocky ridges, long after other hills are forgotten. The whole range is too much for anyone except the hardest walker to complete in one day, but by using Braithwaite as a base then an almost unlimited number of routes can be planned and the following are only included as a guide.

Climb Grisedale Pike by way of the path which starts at the first bend on the Whinlatter road out of Braithwaite. Do

View from Lodore Inn, southern end of Derwent Water

1 Catbells
2 Barf
3 Swinside
4 Binsey
5 Doda
6 Ullock Pike, St Herbert's Isle (below)
7 Longside Edge
8 Carl Side, Carsleddam (below)
   Derwent Isle (still lower)
9 Skiddaw

Derwentwater moorings

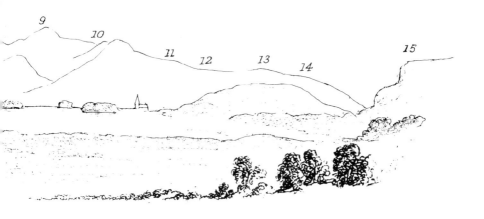

10 Skiddaw Low Man, Lord's Isle
   (below)
11 Jenkin Hill, Rampsholm Isle (below)
12 Walla Crag (below)
13 Lonscale Fell, Latrigg (below)

14 Pike
15 Falcon Crag, Barrow House (below)

Ashness Bridge

H	not go straight up on to the ridge but take the track slanting upwards to the right, as it is much easier. The path climbs on to Sleet How then over Grisedale Pike and on to Hopegill Head. Go left down to Hopegill Hause and either turn left down into Coledale or better still climb Crag Hill and return by way of Scar Crag, Stile End and High Coledale Farm. As an alternative take in Causey Pike above Stair and walk across Scar Crag then turn left over Wanlope to Whiteless Pike and then down into Sail Beck. Turn left here and climb up to the Newlands Pass and catch the mini bus or cross over the col between Sail Beck and Rigg Beck and down to Stair village.
7m	
5h	
****	
oooo	

H	Robinson can be climbed either from Buttermere or from the bottom of Newlands and up Scope Beck. Follow the ridge along from Robinson across Littledale and Hindscarth Edges to Dale Head and down to Dalehead Tarn where a left turn leads into Newlands Beck or right to the top of Honister.
6m	
4½h	
****	
oooo	

H	The best known and best loved walk in Lakeland is without doubt the Cat Bells to High Spy Ridge. It is easy and safe in all but the harshest weather. Take the lake ferry to Hawse End landing stage and climb gently on to Cat Bells. Turn left and follow the heathery moorland way across Hawse Gate, Maiden Moor, High Spy and down to Dale Head. Turn right here and walk down Newlands Beck to Little Town. A wide track follows the base of Cat Bells to Skelgill and Hawse End.
7m	
4½h	
***	
oooo	

Walkers crossing these fells cannot fail to notice traces of mining activity, some old and some new. All this area from Whinlatter to Borrowdale has been extensively mined since German miners were brought over from Augsberg in Elizabethan times to exploit the riches beneath these hills. A wide variety of ores and metals were found ranging from copper, lead, graphite to small amounts of gold and silver. Goldscope mine in New-lands Valley suggest by its name that gold was once found there. Today only barytes is mined at Force Crag Mine beneath Grisedale Pike.

Even though the German miners intermarried with local girls very few of them stayed behind when the mines began to get worked out. Most of them returned to their native Augsberg or moved to the coal mines of South Wales. Possibly the local name Fisher is a derivative of the German Fischer, but any other German sounding names have now long disappeared.

Moot Hall, Keswick

Fitz Park Museum and Art Gallery, Keswick

The buildings were built of Borrowdale stone at the beginning of the twentieth century as a purpose-built museum and art gallery. There are original manuscripts by the Romantic Poets, especially Robert Southey (Poet Laureate 1814-43), plus Wordsworth, Coleridge and Sir Hugh Walpole. A large model of the Lake District made in 1834 is on display, as well as extensive and fine displays of minerals, butterflies and moths. Also on display are fossils, cannons, swords, guns Stone-age axes, Roman remains and the famous musical stones.

Mirehouse, Keswick

A house with many literary connections. Exhibits include manuscripts and pictures relating to Bacon, Tennyson, Carlyle, Fitzgerald and the Lake Poets. Woodland and lakeside walk, access to open-air theatre and a Norman church.

Lingholm, Portinscale, Derwent Water

Formal and woodland gardens, exceptional views of Borrowdale.

Whinlatter Pass Visitor Centre, Thornthwaite Forest (Forestry Commission), 2m west of Braithwaite on Keswick-Cockermouth road (207245)

Displays and audio-visual presentation of man's impact through the ages on the fells and forest. There is a trail from the centre with magnificent views of Bassenthwaite and Derwent Water.

Lorton Hall, Low Lorton, Cockermouth

Part is a pele tower dating from the fifteenth century, most of the rest is medieval with a neo-classical frontage of the seventeenth century. There is fine oak panelling, a priest's hole, Jacobean and Carolean furniture. Open only by prior arrangement.

One product of these hills was graphite and this led to the formation 150 years ago in Keswick, of the Cumberland Pencil Company. Using graphite from Borrowdale and local timber a flourishing industry grew up, but as the graphite is now worked out the firm imports it from Sri Lanka and also the cedar has to be imported from abroad.

Keswick has greatly improved since the controversial A66 was diverted around the town. At one time life was becoming unbearable as huge lorries tried to get round the corner by the centuries old Royal Oak Hotel into the market square where the Old Moot Hall still stands. There is an information centre on the ground floor of the town hall run by the lake District National Park.

Guided walks, both low and high level are organised in Keswick and usually start from the information centre. The extensive programme starts quite early in the season. Climbing Guides are also available to lead or instruct mountaineers on local climbs of all standards. Information about them can be found either at the information centre or by enquiring at Fishers Mountaineering Equipment shop.

Keswick has become a busy tourist town with hotels and guest houses ranging upwards to the highest standard. Its amenities include a theatre, cinema, public park and the Fitz Park Museum, which has an interesting collection of manuscripts of the Romantic poets like Robert Southey and also a small selection of Wordsworth's original papers. There is an interesting large scale model of the Lake District in the museum, but perhaps the most unique exhibits are the musical stones collected by the Richardson family. Up the road a little way from Fitz Park and inside the now defunct Keswick railway station is a fine model railway layout.

The little mountain between Keswick and Skiddaw with its smooth grassy top and wooded sides is Latrigg, which has long been a favourite of locals as well as visitors. The beauty of Latrigg is that it can be climbed in the odd hour or so on the first or last day of a holiday. Or maybe if the early part of the day has been wet then Latrigg will make the best of an otherwise spoilt day. To get to Latrigg follow the river downstream through Fitz Park and turn right past the hospital and right again, then left into Spooney Green Lane. From Spooney Green follow a path that climbs up through the woods beneath Mallen Dodd, but before it reaches Gale Road turn right and gently ascend to the grassy summit of Latrigg. Hopefully the weather will be clear enough for a wonderful view of Derwent Water. From the top continue eastwards until you meet a track which gradually improves in surface and then turns right to drop down through Brundholme Wood back to Keswick.

M
3½m
2h
**
ooo

One of the major attractions of Keswick is Derwent Water, a lake of many faces with a long and interesting history. Rowing boats and motor boats can be hired from the landing stage at the end of the side road off the Borrowdale Road. Also this is where the ferries which ply on a round-the-lake route start and finish. The local sailing club facilities are across on the Portinscale side. The Century Theatre complex on Lake Road produce a wide range of shows throughout the year, ranging from ballet to plays and concerts.

The most famous viewpoint for Derwent Water is Castlehead. The approach is from the old Ambleside road outside Keswick. The land, like much around Derwent Water, is preserved for ever by the National Trust. From Friars Crag, a little way beyond the ferry landing, all four of the Derwent islands are in view. Friars Crag is the subject of countless photographs and paintings and it is supposed to be the place where monks set off for the most southerly island, St Herberts, where at one time its shrine was a place of pilgrimage.

Derwent Island was once owned by the monks of Furness Abbey and later by German miners. Still later it came into the hands of the ill-fated Earls of Derwentwater. The family supported the Stuart cause and the last earl was beheaded for supporting the 1715 rebellion. It is said that following the execution there was a great display of Northern Lights which afterwards became known as Lord Derwentwater's Lights.

Only four islands are shown on even the largest scale maps, but there is often a fifth. This is the famous floating island, a curious floating mass of vegetation which appears occasionally in the still waters of the bay opposite the Lodore Hotel about the middle of October.

It is possible to walk right round Derwent Water by starting at the bridge beyond the pencil factory and taking the path leading to Portinscale. Turn left out of the village on the Stair road to Derwent Bank where a path leads on through Lingholme woods to Hawse End. Turn left and follow the lake shore all the way through Manesty Park and across the swampy area around Great Bay and over the River Derwent to join the Borrowdale road by the Lodore Hotel. One can either catch the ferry here, or follow the road until it is possible to walk on the lake shore to Calfclose Bay. A path leads across nearby fields to Friars Crag and Keswick. The gardens at Lingholme, which are open to the public, specialise in rhododendrons and azaleas in a forest

L
9½
4½
**
oo(

setting. The magnificent view up Borrowdale from Lingholme is at its best in early June when the shrubs are in flower.

It is difficult to decide which of the Borrowdale villages is the most attractive, as they are all in their own individual ways equally delightful. All cater for the inner-man and are therefore useful starting or finishing places for anyone exploring the fells or lower levels of Borrowdale.

L
5½m
3h
***
ooo

One of the most famous walks in the area starts at Grange and climbs gradually to the south through Dalt Wood to Castle Crag and on to Seatoller. The return route is through Johnny's Wood to Longthwaite and Rosthwaite, and follows the river back to Grange.

Castle Crag is worth a special visit. The name comes from the ancient fort which once adorned its easily defended summit. A couple of caves nearby in the old High Hows quarry were the summer home of Millican Dalton an eccentric mountaineer of prewar days.

At the top of the Honister road from Seatoller, at over 1,100 ft above sea level, the green slate quarry makes a good starting point for a number of high level routes. The easiest way up Great Gable starts here and follows an old smugglers track known as Moses Trod. Moses was an illicit whisky maker who had his still hidden beneath the Napes Crags on

H
6m
4h
****
oooo

Gable. To join Moses' Trod climb up to the ruins of the old drum house once used to lower stone down to Honister. Turn left and take an easy climb across the flank of Fleetwith and beneath Brandreth to Stone Cove. Go right to Beck Head and then steeply left up to the summit of Great Gable and the memorial to members of the Fell and Rock Climbing Club who were killed in World War I. A Rememberance Service is held here every November in homage to the men who gave their lives so that others can enjoy the mountains they loved. Drop down the rough rocky path from the top of Great Gable to Windy Gap and up to Green Gable to continue over Brandreth and Grey Knotts back to Honister.

Another way to climb Gable is from Seathwaite. The route follows Sourmilk Gill up to the slopes leading to the summit of Green Gable and then to Great Gable. The descent is down to Sty Head, and then take a left turn to follow an easy path by Styhead Tarn and its emptying stream to Airy's Bridge, where a right turn leads round to Stockley Bridge and back to Seathwaite.

H
5½m
4h
****
oooo

The sturdy farm buildings of Seathwaite have weathered many storms and floods. This is the wettest place in England with an annual rainfall of 131 inches. Seathwaite is the usual start for a climb of Scafell Pike from the north. Rather than follow the main path on the east side of the stream, try the other bank which is a much less used route. Go through the archway between the barns, cross the footbridge and turn sharp left and eventually climb the rough track above the splashing sounds of Taylorforce Gill. Continue on to Sty Head and climb Scafell by the Corridor Route (see Chapter 4). Return across Broad Crag and Great End and turn left towards Sprinkling Tarn, but before reaching the tarn turn right down Grains Gill to Stockley Bridge and Stonethwaite.

H
9m
6h
****
oooo

An alternative walk avoiding Scafell is to follow the route from Seathwaite as far as Sty Head and then turn left to Sprinkling Tarn and left again down Langstrath Beck to Stonethwaite.

H
9m
5h
***
ooo

The golden eagle is slowly returning to these high fells after being extinct for years and can occasionally be seen, but do not mistake a Buzzard for one — they are similar but smaller. Eagle Crag at the junction of Langstrath with Greenup Gill is supposed to be where the last eagle was shot in the less enlightened days of the last century. Parish records tell of large numbers of eagles slain beween 1713 and 1765 and there was a rope kept in

Friars Crag, Derwentwater

Bowder Stone, Borrowdale

Borrowdale for the express purpose of lowering young men down the rocks to destroy their nests.

Many huge boulders were left behind by the retreating glaciers, but none is so well known as the Bowder Stone. One wonders if the stone would be so well known if it was perched up a side valley and not convenient to the road and car park? Even with the popularity of this small section of Borrowdale, careful screening and footpath maintenance by the National Trust ensures that it will always be attractive. The fellside above was purchased as a memorial to King Edward VII and is now known as Kings How. From the Bowder Stone car park a path wanders through the woods past the stone and down to the road. After about 100 yd leave the road at a gate and stile on the left and climb the bracken covered slopes directly to the top of Kings How. Return by going downhill, then left and back to the car park to complete an easy mountaineering expedition.

M
2m
2h
**
oooo

Even though it is necessary to pay for the privilege of viewing the Lodore Falls, it is money well spent but only after a period of heavy rain. They do have a habit of drying to a mere trickle in drought conditions. Walk up to the falls and continue through Lodore Woods to join the Watendlath road back and over Ashness Bridge for a walk of surprise views. Some are well known, but all are superlative. For a longer walk from Ashness, continue beyond Low Strutta and across the top of the rock climbers' paradise of crags and into Keswick.

M
2½m
2h
**
ooo
5m
3h
***
ooc

The 'hidden valley' sheltering the hamlet of Watendlath was used by Sir Hugh Walpole, who lived by the side of Derwentwater, as the setting for *Rogue Herries* and *Judith Paris*, the latter giving a graphic description of sunshine and storm in this place. *Fortress* and *Vanessa* complete the quartet of Walpole's novels based on the Lake District. Four old and well known paths leave Watendlath which were used as the routes in and out

Derwentwater

of the village long before people walked for pleasure. One of them is an easy walk up and over the moors to Thirlmere, and half way down hill the path skirts Harrop Tarn.

Thirlmere was the first of Manchester's Lakeland reservoirs, first used in 1879, but it is only recently that they have allowed access into its surrounding woods and forest. There is a nature trail around Launchy Gill and another on the far side near Wythburn. The motor road on the west side makes a pleasing alternative to the busy A591. Look out for red squirrels here and the woodland birds attracted by the nesting boxes provided by a thoughtful authority.

From the northern end of the lake a steep path up between Raven Crag and Smaithwaite Banks leads to a prehistoric fort on Castle Crag. The view is enough to explain why our forefathers chose this spot for their protection in time of trouble.

The landlord of the King's Head at Thirlspot on the A591 regularly white-washes stones to mark the track via Browncove Crags to the top of Helvellyn. Perhaps one should rather say the track down from Helvellyn to his pub for the stones lead directly to this haven and who can deny such harmless advertising?

The rocky low mass of High Rigg which divides St John's Vale from Nadder Beck is used in autumn for hound trailing based on Dale Bottom Farm. The trail is laid by dragging a rag soaked in a blend of aniseed and paraffin along the route and the hounds follow this at tremendous speed.

From Dale Bottom a path leads to the old Keswick-Penrith road and Castlerigg Stone Circle. Although not as complex as Stonehenge its setting is far more dramatic than its southern counterpart. Threlkeld, now thankfully bypassed by the 'new' A66, shelters beneath huge Blencathra and is home for shepherds and quarrymen. Also this is where the famous Blencathra Foxhounds live when they are not out chasing foxes over the

Watendlath

hills. Threlkeld is supposed to be named after Thorgell a Viking who settled here and created his Thorskeld or Thor's clearing. There is the story of a skull once kept in a small dark room at Threlkeld Place which would not stay buried. Every time the tenant either buried it or even threw it out into the sea it always managed to return home before he did. The only answer to the problem came when the farmer bricked it up and left the house.

Saddleback is the modern name for Blencathra, but according to the Ordnance Survey the name is Hallsfell Top! Most climbers prefer the old name of Blencathra, it sounds much more in keeping with this giant who shelters Threlkeld from the cold north winds. The easy way up is from the old Blencathra Sanatorium (now an outdoor pursuits centre) and up the never ending grassy slope of Blease Fell and return the same way. A much more exciting route however goes up the face of Halls' Fell and across the narrow, but easy rockridge directly to the summit. Return with care down Sharp Edge and round the breast of the fell to the road at Scales.

H
7m
4h
***
oo

H
4m
4h
****
oooo

Walkers crossing the saddle beyond the summit of Blencathra will notice a cross made of white stones which were originally laid out by Harold Robbins of Threlkeld in memory of a now forgotten walker who died here. The cross has been extended since then by visitors who continue where Mr Robbins left off. Beneath the eastern crags of Blencathra is Scales Tarn where according to tradition two massive and uncaught fishes live.

The last mountain in this northern section has almost been made an island by the River Glendermachin which practically goes full circle in its course before running to the west and eventually into Bassenthwaite Lake. This is Southern Fell where on the eve of Midsummer's Day in 1745 at least twenty-six trustworthy people witnessed a ghost army marching over its steep sides. When they went to look the next day, there was absolutely no trace of anyone, let alone an army. Subsequent news reported that Bonnie Prince Charlie had been manoeuvring his troops far away across the Solway Firth prior to marching on London. The only explanation was that the rebels were reflected on to Southern Fell in a kind of mirage.

(overleaf) *Castlerigg stone circle*

7 Ullswater to Penrith

The broad grassy slopes of the Helvellyn/Fairfield range which fall smoothly towards the A591 provide the western boundary of this final section of the Lake District. Their eastern faces are much more interesting, being mainly composed of steep rocky coves carved by ancient glaciers.

To the north the land is wild and desolate, but the gem of the district is the central valley flooded by Ullswater, a lake of many moods. East of the lake is almost unknown territory to the average visitor. Large areas are given over to deer forest, usually undisturbed by the sight or sound of man. Curlew haunt the ridges of the High Street Range where the final outliers of the Lake District dip their feet in Manchester's Hawswater Reservoir.

The bleak pastures around the A66 produce some of the best Lakeland sheep which are sold at the market near the old Troutbeck station. The main breeds are Herdwick and Swaledales. These are bred mainly for their wool and are hardy enough to stay out on high pastures in the worst weather.

The railway which once linked Penrith to Keswick and the western coast is now no more, and it suffered the final indignity by having sections of its track used to carry the improved main road to the industrial Cumbrian coast.

Bleak though these pastures might be, the road through is bounded by inspiring distant views of higher hills to the south and east. Nearer to hand are the conical humps of Great and Little Mell Fell. The A5091 winds its way through Dockray before the steep descent to Ullswater and a back lane turns off from the centre of the village to climb a little way up Aira Beck on the right. Onwards is the route of the old coach road from Penrith to Keswick. This road is now a neglected track, but once it was the main route into northern Lakeland from Penrith. The old road can be included in an easy ten-mile

View from the Matterdale Road above Ullswater

1 Place Fell
2 Cockley How
3 Arnison Crag
4 Dove Crag

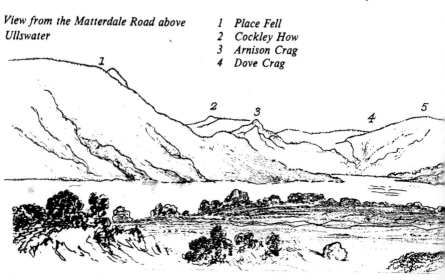

108

H
10m
5h
***
ooo

walk from near Dockray. It starts at High Row and follows the coach road to the ford across Groove Beck. Turn left beyond the stream and climb the gradually steepening Matterdale Common to Great Dod. Keep right at the summit and walk down beside the infant Mosedale Beck, crossing its many tributaries on the way to Mariel Bridge. Turn right here along the coach road back to High Row. In all probability the only people you will meet on this walk in a lesser known part of the fells are shepherds, or other fell walkers with a desire to escape the more crowded areas.

L
2m
1h
*
oooo

On the way down to Ullswater, the road passes through Glencoyne Park where there is one of the prettiest and unspoilt waterfalls in the region. Park the car in the Aira Point Car Park and walk upstream to the sylvan dash of Aira Force and its nearby companion High Force. Wordsworth was so moved by its delights as to use this little valley as the setting for his poem *The Somnambulist*, a romantic legend which ends in sadness. Set in medieval times it concerns, Emma the pretty daughter of a nearby lord of the manor, who fretted for her lover away on a crusade. After months of pining she began to walk in her sleep and one night fell into the torrent. As in all true stories her lover came back just at that moment and she lived just long enough to recognise him. The story ends with the knight ending his days as a hermit in a nearby cave.

M
3½m
2½h
**
ooo

After visiting the falls you can either continue up through the wooded valley to Dockray or turn right at the top of Aira Force and follow the track through deer forest and over the summit of Gowbarrow Fell. Return by continuing across the fell and down to the shooting box by the side of a track which gently follows the contours above Yew Crag and its views across Ullswater. Rest awhile here, and drop down to the car park beyond Lyulph's Tower, built on the site of an ancient pele-tower, once home of Lyulph first Lord of Ullswater

It was on the shore of Ullswater beneath Gowbarrow Fell that Dorothy Wordsworth saw the daffodils which were later immortalised by her brother William. In her words they 'seemed as if they verily laughed with the wind'. Daffodils still laugh with the wind and Gowbarrow Woods are filled with flowers every spring.

5 *Birks, Hall Bank (below)*
6 *St Sunday Crag, Grisedale (below)*
7 *Fairfield*
8 *Glenridding Dod*

9 *Black Crag*
10 *Glencoyne Wood (below)*
11 *Sheffield Pike, Glencoyne (below)*
12 *Gowbarrow Park*

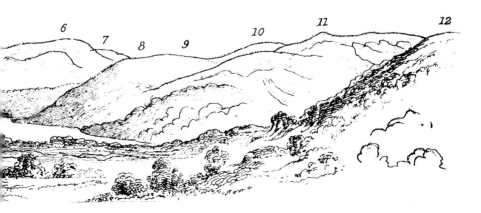

Aira Force, Ullswater

The road from Pooley Bridge to Patterdale (or Patrick's Dale as translated from the Irish-Norse) hugs the Ullswater shore all the way to Saint Patrick's landing where boats propelled by engine or manpower can be hired by the hour or the day. The fishing is good, especially in the deep waters off the various rocky promontories which jut out into the lake. The *Raven* and its sister the *Lady of the Lake* between them run three scheduled trips each day both ways from Glenridding Pier to Pooley Bridge. Both venerable ships are now fitted with diesel engines, but were originally steamers. The *Raven* was built in 1889 but its older sister the *Lady of the Lake* has had a chequered life of more than a century.

She was twice sunk at her moorings and once damaged by fire while out of the water undergoing an annual refit, but she is now fully renovated and hopefully will ply up and down the lake for many more years to come. As well as operating as ferries the boats do round-the-lake cruises and can be chartered for private trips and dances.

The twin villages of Glenridding and Patterdale make an ideal centre for exploring the waterways and fells of Eastern Lakeland. Hotels, rented cottages, campsites and the specially designed Youth Hostel by Goldrill Beck cater for all age groups and pockets.

The district is especially suitable for pony trekking along the old bridle roads which abound locally. Tracks such as the one across the Sticks Pass make a fine expedition. This old way climbs up past the remains of extensive lead mining industry to zig-zag its way up Stang End and then up to the summit of the pass and beyond. The name of the pass comes from the early method of guiding the pony drovers when they were the commercial life blood of the remoter parts of England.

Few who visit Patterdale fail to be drawn by the allure of Helvellyn and especially to climb it by first crossing Striding Edge. To some Striding Edge holds a good deal of terror, but with care the ridge is an easy scramble with most of its difficult bits easily avoided by turning to their right, or northern side. The only tricky part is on the final tower before the last climb up to the top of Helvellyn. The faint hearted are usually spared the horror of finding the memorial to the hunter who in 1858 fell into Nethermost Cove while following the local fox hounds. Once on the broad summit of Helvellyn the angle of the climb eases so much that in 1926 an aeroplane landed and took off again without encountering any problems. There is a plaque recording this, but regretably the message must be de-

H
3m
3h
***
ooo

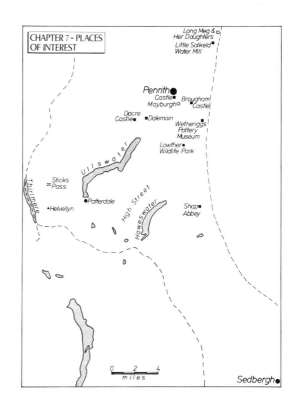

CHAPTER 7 – PLACES OF INTEREST

Long Meg & Her Daughters
Little Salkeld Water Mill

Penrith
Castle
Mayburgh
Brougham Castle

Dacre Castle
Dalemain
Wetheriggs Pottery Museum

Lowther Wildlife Park

Thirlmere

Sticks Pass

Helvellyn

Ullswater

Patterdale

High Street

Haweswater

Shap Abbey

0   2   4
miles

Sedbergh

St Patrick's Landing, Ullswater

ciphered from the holes which once held the letters in place, as either frost or vandals have caused their disappearance. The third memorial on this summit tells the story of a faithful sheep dog which stayed with its master for several weeks after he fell to his death below by Red Tarn in 1890.

Dogs have long featured in the history of Helvellyn. High grazing sheep are rounded up in spring and moved to valley areas around the farmsteads for lambing and later on for shearing. The hounds of the Ullswater pack also cross Helvellyn's broad flanks. Sometimes strays from the hunt remain around the summit cairn and spend a glorious summer begging scraps from visitors. Charming and friendly though the hounds might be, it is wrong to feed them (and this also applies to sheep), as they soon lose the desire to return home and also the ability to fend for themselves in high places. Once summer has gone and with it their free handouts, the hounds make their way home to the kennels, but as they can no longer keep up with the rest of the pack, they are of no further use to the hunt and their usual fate is to be put down.

H
4m
2h
***
ooo

From the top of Helvellyn the choices of descent back to Glenridding are to either continue northwards, turning to the right either down Swirral Edge or to go on as far as Whiteside and down Red Screes into Glenriddings Beck and the lead mine road. The longest route, but probably the most interesting is south over Dollywaggon Pike to Grisedale Tarn and left to follow the bridleway down Grisedale into Patterdale.

H
6m
3h
***
oooo

The middle section of the valley of Glenridding will appeal to industrial archaeologists but probably few others. The whole of the northern side of the valley beneath Stang End is a devastating ruin of the lead mining industry which once provided employment for scores of men and support for their families.

The road continuing southwards from Ullswater follows the short, narrow, flat alluvial plain to Brothers Water. Fields in this plain provide a scant harvest of hay which must be quickly gathered between showers to feed sheep and cattle in the hard winters which hit Patterdale in most years. Beyond Brothers Water the road rises steeply to the top of the Kirkstone Pass and its inn. Today the road surface is smoothly metalled and the modern motor car climbs the gradient with energy to spare, but spare a thought to travellers who once came this way in horsedrawn vehicles. Then the inn at the top of the pass really proved its worth. Not for them the leisurely drive, but usually a hard push behind the coach! If conditions were bad and the coach heavily laden it was not uncommon for some of the passengers to be forced to help the horses.

The fells west of Kirkstone are best approached from the beautiful valley of Dovedale beyond the sixteenth-century farm house called Hartsop Hall. The path keeps well away from the valley fields at first and skirts a hazel wood before climbing up by the side of Dove Falls and into the rocky fastness of Houndshope Cove. Massive boulders in the cove are thought to be of volcanic origin and make for an interesting afternoon's exploration. Some are so big that their flat tops are covered by small gardens of lush grasses and sub-alpine plants.

H
6m
4h
***
ooo

Above Houndshope Cove the climbing angle eases on to Dove Crag, part of the Fairfield Horseshoe. Here a decision has to be made to turn right or left? The shorter route is to the left across Black Brow and Little Hart Crag and down to the col of Scandale Pass then left to follow Caiston Beck to Hartsop Hall. For a longer walk from Dove Crag, turn right to climb Hart Crag and then on to Fairfield. A right turn to the north east follows the narrow heights of the ridge over

H
9m
6h
***
ooo

Deepdale Hause then on to the oddly named St Sunday Crag and steeply down its north-east ridge to Patterdale.

East and north of the Kirkstone the remote hills do not have the same crowded summits as are found in the central areas. These hills and moors are the haunt of wild birds and give sanctuary to herds of red deer. Remote and beautiful tarns fill hidden combes — tarns offering sport to the angler prepared to walk across hard moorland with effort rewarded at the end.

H
5 m
3½ h
****
ooo

The easiest approaches to these far eastern fells is from height gained by road to the top of the Kirkstone. An easy climb from the inn leads to St Ravens Edge and on to John Bell's Banner (marked as Caudale Moor on some maps). On to Stony Cove Pike and then down to the col of Threshthwaite Mouth. Turn left here down the wild descent to Threshthwaite Cove and follow Pasture Beck to Hartsop and the road where a bus can be caught back to Kirkstone if the car was left up there.

Beyond Threshthwaite Mouth the whole long range of High Street opens up to the north east. The Romans used this as a safe high level route for their road to Penrith. Their interest was in safety from attack by the wild tribes hiding in the many remote valleys and combes along the way. No doubt the weather could still be treacherous in those days and one can only wonder how many footsloggers were trapped in winter storms on these heights.

The length of High Street to Pooley Bridge makes a long hard day's expedition, but one which leaves the walker

H
14 m
8 h
****
ooo

with a real sense of achievement. Start in Patterdale and follow the path above Side Farm and meander upwards to Angle Tarn and reach High Street by way of the Knott. Turn left here and follow in the footsteps of Roman legionnaires across High Raise, Raven Howe and Wether Hill (a wether is a gelded ram).

Next aim for a lone chimney standing on the side of Loadpot Hill; this is all that remains of the former shooting lodge known as Lowther House. Once over Loadpot the track gently descends all the way to Pooley Bridge, but look out for a complicated junction of tracks beyond the Stone Circle marked as 'The Cockpit' on OS maps. Turn left here and make for Roehead Farm before joining the lane into Pooley Bridge.

Early Britons attached great importance to this north-eastern moorland and the whole area is studded with their cairns, standing stones and circles. What is now land inhabited by a few farms and the occasional small village would once have supported large numbers of our emerging forefathers. High Street has long featured in the history of the eastern Lake District. Ancient Britons gave way to Romans who in turn left their handiwork to an appreciative invader from the north. The Street was used regularly by border rovers right down to the eighteenth century. Sheep and cattle stealers from Southern Scotland were trounced on its heights. The route became part of a drove way in more settled times when fat cattle were walked from the Highlands to southern markets. Shepherds used High Street as a meeting place to return straying animals to their rightful owners. The meet eventually became something of a fair and horse racing was regularly held on the summit.

The crags and ridges east of High Street are best approached from Hawswater. From Gatesgarth Pass two short and two long ridges cut sharply into the fell sides. The first section creates the combe holding Small Water, next comes Blea Water bounded on its north side by Long Stile and then wider Riggindale with Kidsty Pike to the north. All this is fascinating country well justifying several day's exploration. A round trip taking in all the wild features starts at Hawswater road end and climbs up by Small Water

View from the old quarry at Blowick on Ullswater

1 Place Fell	6 Arnison Crag
2 Hartsop Dodd	7 Birks
3 Caudale Moor	8 St Sunday Crag
4 Kirkstone Pass	9 Grisedale House
5 Cockley How, Deep Dale Park (below)	10 Tarn Crag
	11 Dollywaggon Pike, Grisedale (below)

H
6m
4h
****
ooo

to Nan Bield Pass to turn right across Mardale Ill Bell and on to High Street. Long Stile makes the best line of descent, with excellent aerial views of Blea Water on the right and Riggindale on the left.

When Hawswater was made, the reservoir engineers flooded the valley of Mardale and drowned a village which once sheltered outlaws. Mardale had a line of 'Kings' which lasted until 1885. The first of them in 1209 was Hugh Holme who was suspected of plotting against King John. Hugh was forced to take refuge in a cave above Riggindale until after the king's death. Hugh remained an outlaw and became a law to himself, creating the dynasty which became known as the 'Kings of Mardale'.

Valleys draining north into Ullswater from the High Street range contain the Martindale Deer Forest. The boundaries of the forest are defined by a fence enclosing the upper reaches of the Rampsgill and Bannerdale valleys. However deer are skilled at jumping the highest

fence and they roam freely well beyond its confines. The forest is their sanctuary and on no account should it be entered without permission. The red deer have been established here for centuries and have provided both legal and illegal meat for people living around the forest. Old records tell of deer poaching and the harsh justice handed out to captured poachers. Across in Wet Sleddale towards Shap are the stone ruins of an old deer trap into which the herd would be driven for sorting and culling for winter meat.

The only rights of way surrounding Martindale are the High Street path to the east and a series of tracks radiating from Boardale Hause. The usual approach is by the track up from Patterdale via Side Farm and then either across Bedafell to Dale Head, or down Boardale to the road end. Both routes link to follow the road to Howtown and the ferry landing stage for the return to Glenridding and Patterdale. An alter-

H
5m
3h
***
ooo

H
5m
4h
***
oooo

native from Boardale Hause turns hard left and climbs Place Fell before dropping down to Sandwick and the lake shore. This is a delightful walk and a full day should be allowed if you are to appreciate all the scenery. The journey back alongside Ullswater is the particular high light of a magnificent excursion of fell and lake views.

Lake steamers ply almost into the quiet village of Pooley Bridge at the northern end of Ullswater. The pier is as close to the lake outlet as navigation allows.

L
4m
1½h
**
ooo

Beyond is the stately home of Dalemain which can be reached from Pooley Bridge by a riverside path which starts across the river from the village. To get to Dalemain by this route, follow the river Eamont as far as the A592 Penrith road and turn left along it to a cross roads. A right turn along a cart track leads directly into Dalemain. Return along the A592 for about a quarter of a mile and then turn left across the river. The path follows a line a little way in from the river before

entering Pooley Bridge by way of Hole House Farm. Another easy walk from Pooley Bridge follows the Hole House Farm path, but instead of crossing the river continue on to the village of Barton. Turn right here and by lanes and footpath walk to Cellerton. Continue southwards to join the High Street track before Winder Hall and make two right turns to join a path down to Cracoe and the road back to Pooley Bridge.

L
5m
2h
***
oo

Dalemain House started life as a fortified pele tower in the twelfth century and later more peaceable generations of the Hassall family extended it until it took on the present imposing facade in the Georgian style. Inside the house is the museum of the Westmorland and Cumberland Yeomanry and outside is a deer-park and Country Life Museum.

As happened to Kendal, the M6 motorway has made a vast improvement to Penrith. No longer are its streets clogged all night and day with heavy traffic, and now the town has reverted to the sleepy

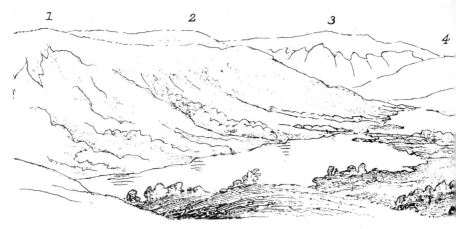

View from Burn Banks, near the foot of Haweswater
(Note that Haweswater now covers a larger area than depicted here.)

PLACES TO VISIT NEAR PENRITH:

Dalemain House, Pooley, on Penrith-Ullswater road.
Originally built in the twelfth century with medieval, Elizabethan and Georgian additions, and an imposing facade built in 1740. There is a comprehensive collection of furniture and pictures, gardens, parkland and country life museum. Westmorland and Cumberland Yeomanry Regimental Museum.

Brougham Castle (Dept of Environment), 1½ m east of Penrith
Erected on site of Roman fort of Brocavum. One of the most interesting castle ruins in northern England, consisting of a keep built about 1176 and later buildings.

Penrith Castle
The ruins of a fourteenth-century defence against Scottish raids, lived in by Warwick the Kingmaker and the Duke of Gloucester, later Richard III. In a public park.

Hutton-in-the-Forest, 5 m north west of Penrith
Fourteenth-century pele tower with later additions, containing beautiful carvings, plasterwork ceilings, tapestries, furniture, paintings, china and armour. Gardens, woods and lake.

Dacre Castle, northern end of Ullswater
Massive fourteenth-century pele tower restored in 1675. Open by written appointment only.

Lowther Wildlife Country Park, 4 m south of Penrith, near A6
A 150-acre park, part of Earl of Lonsdale's estates, with a wide collection of European animals and birds, which either roam freely or are housed in special enclosures.

Shap Abbey (Dept of Environment), 1 m west of Shap village
Built by Premonstratensian canons about 1201 who moved here from Preston Patrick near Kendal. The great West Tower remains, as well as the ruined walls and foundations of the rest of the buildings, which was abandoned about 1540.

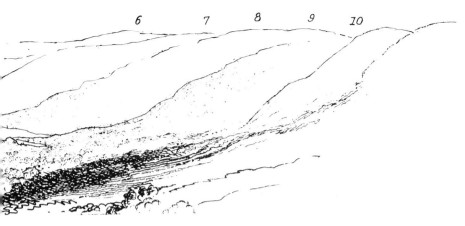

1 Swindale Common	6 High Street
2 Branstree	7 Kidsey Pike
3 Harter Fell	8 Low Raise
4 Nan Bield and pass into Kentmere Riggindale Crag (below)	9 Raven How
5 Piot Crag, Castle Crag (2nd line below)	10 Measand Beck (below)

Dalemain House

market it was before the advent of the juggernaut. Penrith has had a turbulent and long history. All round it are remains of perhistoric tumuli and henges, some linked with legends lost in antiquity. King Arthur is reputed to keep watch with his knights by his Round Table at nearby Eamont Bridge.

Sir Lancelot du Lac killed the giant Torquin who is buried in the churchyard in Penrith Parish Church. The grave is marked by two badly worn upright stones and four incised semi-circular stones set in pairs between the uprights. There has been much conjecture over the years about the origin of the stones, but perhaps they are best explained as being relics of an ancient religion which was assimilated by the 'new' Christian faith. Early attempts to carve the uprights into the shape of the cross have now almost worn away and the stones remain an enigma.

Two Roman roads joined here; one from the fort of Ravenglass and the other from the east by way of Stainmore. The Romans built their fort of Brocavum a mile or so downstream along the river Eamont from Penrith. Later in the twelfth century Brougham Castle was erected to guard the Stainmore road. It later fell into disuse until 1651 when Lady Anne Clifford, who had a romantic passion for rebuilding ancient monuments, had it renovated.

Standing stones in Penrith churchyard

During the bloody days of border warfare, Penrith was burnt down several times, the worst devastation was when Black Douglas descended on the town in 1347. Not content with laying the place to waste the Scots took away every able bodied survivor as their prisoners. Traces of yards can still be seen where like at Kendal the townsfolk were able to lock up their livestock and valuables in case of night attack from the Scots.

The castle was built in 1399 by William Strickland, Bishop of Carlisle, and it has links with England's royal history. It was once the home of the young Richard Duke of Gloucester who later became Richard III and died on Bosworth field. His dying words, immortalised by Shakespeare, offered his whole kingdom in return for a horse on which to escape.

Leaving the rushing traffic to the motorway, the A6 is again a pleasant highway south. Unlike the motorway it has the advantage of allowing drivers to stop and detour down side roads leading to all manner of interesting places.

About 4 miles south of Penrith is a wild life park set in 150 acres of Lowther Park.

Penrith Castle

The animals and birds are mainly of European origin and as a result are on display with the minimum of restrictions. Lowther Castle is home of the Earl of Lonsdale. When, in 1683, the first Lord Lonsdale was developing the estate and wanted to build a church he discovered that the village of Lowther was in the way, he simply built a new village, Lowther Newtown, and moved all the inhabitants.

Hawswater now covering the drowned site of Mardale, is approached by several miles of winding roads. The head of the reservoir is the best starting point for fell walks and climbs on the outliers of High Street, but it is also worth the journey just for the solitude and scenery of the fells on either side. Hawswater has a good stock of char and other fresh water fish. Permits, both day and season, can be bought locally at the hotel. There is a path on the far side of the reservoir, but unless you can arrange to be met by transport at the other end, the walk back along the road, even with the views, can be a little tedious.

Shap is another much quieter spot since they built the M6 motorway. The village stands astride the road as a home for the quarrymen who work the hard granite of the Shap quarries.

The ancient ruins of Shap Abbey are not well signposted, but the journey down the little side road from Shap village to the quiet dignity of the abbey set beside the river Lowther is more than worth while. It was built by the Premonstratensian canons in the twelfth century, and although now only the walls of the west tower remain, the foundations and outline of most of the other parts are visible and indicate its former size.

From the abbey a short path leads over the fields to Keld where its sixteenth-century chapel is now owned by the National Trust. The walk can be extended by returning along a path through Thornship then left towards Shap village and left again towards the lane leading down to the abbey. Even older are a line of boulders, beginning with the Thunder Stone, a little way above the abbey. These

L
2m
1h
**
ooo

119

Shap Abbey

discerning enough to explore off the beaten track.

Travellers passing through the Lune Gap on the M6 near Tebay cannot help being intrigued by the fells which rear up on either side of the motorway. To the west, and bisected by another Borrowdale, are Bretherdale and Roundthwaite Commons on its northern side and Whinfell Common as its southerly boundary. The ridgewalk across Ashtead Fell, Mabbin Crag, Castle Fell, Whinfell Beacon and Grayrigg Common is a delightful ridgewalk which connects the A6 and the A685. The problem with this walk is that it requires transport at either end and unless the walker has an understanding companion or can arrange to start from the opposite end to a friend who also has a car and will swap keys in the middle, then this can become a long and tedious route.

H
5m
4h
***
ooo

The fells east of the motorway are the Howgills, and these offer more scope for walks which start and finish at the same place. Start at Sedbergh for walks along the tops or at Tebay for walks along the long valleys which drain northwards into the infant Lune.

Westmorland and Yorkshire share a common boundary which follows the watershed across the middle of these hills —hills which are covered by a short springy turf, the delight of everyone who treads their summits. These fells are on the boundary of Lakeland and the Yorkshire Dales, but unlike either, they are unspoilt and provide unlimited scope for the walker and nature lover. The latter will find rare sub-alpine plants in the sheltered recesses of the high valleys, or can watch the soaring flight of the buzzard as it lazily scans the fellside for its food.

Sedbergh is the main town in the area, with good simple accommodation readily available and two caravan sites nearby. The boys of Sedbergh's famous school have a tradition of being introduced early

are the remains of an avenue of stones leading into a stone circle a mile south of Shap.

There are few paths across the fells to the west of the A6, and those that are there are long distance routes from one valley to another. These were the short cuts when feet or hooves were the sole means of transport, but they will reward the energetic explorer who wishes to open up new ground for himself. The routes are long, but careful planning beforehand will ensure that strategically parked transport is available for the return home in the evening.

South across the summit of the Shap road are a series of valleys draining to the south east. Some go into the Lune, but most go into the Kent. These are remote valleys not often visited and all are waiting to offer their charms to whoever is to the love of fellwalking. Their 'own' hill is Winder and the sign of Sedbergh pointing 'To the Fell' actually means 'To Winder'. It is an easy hill, which can be taken in its own right or used as a stepping stone to explore the whole mass of fells beyond.

There are only a handful of paths across the Howgills but there is free access and routes which start at Sedbergh can easily be extended to wander all day and then return by one of the southerly valleys which lead to the Kirby Stephen or Tebay road. From Sedbergh the A684 runs through undulating country to cross the M6 close by Killington Reservoir before entering Kendal. But perhaps that is where we came in!

Thunder Stone, Shap

Recommended Walks

SIX LOWER LEVEL WALKS

1 Skelwith Bridge, Little Langdale, Elterwater (p 41)
2 Newlands Beck, Dale Head, High Spy, Maiden Moor (p 96)
3 Grange in Borrowdale, Castle Crag, Seatoller, Rosthwaite, High Hawswood Grange (p 99)
4 Loughrigg Terrace and Fell (p 38)
5 Near Sawrey, Wise Eens Tarn, Claife Woods, Far Sawrey (p 50)
6 The east bank of Ullswater from Patterdale returning by lake steamer from Howtown Wyke (p 110)

SIX HIGH LEVEL WALKS

1 The Fairfield Horseshoe from Rydal (p 34)
2 Helvellyn by Striding Edge and Swirral Edge (p 110)
3 Scafell Pikes by the Corridor Route from Borrowdale (p 70)
4 Red Pike, High Stile from Buttermere (p 86)
5 Grisedale Pike, Coledale Hause, Crag Hill, Causey Pike (p 96)
6 Great Gable by the Climbers' Traverse from Sty Head (p 99)

Further Information for Visitors

The information here has been obtained partly from the leaflets produced by the Cumbria Tourist Board. Admission charges have not been included as they are subject to revision, so check with the local Information Centres.

BUILDINGS AND GARDENS OPEN TO THE PUBLIC

Details are correct at time of publication, but they are subject to modification without notice and intending visitors should always check locally beforehand.

Belle Isle
Bowness on Windermere (394965)
Tel: Windermere 3353
Open: mid May-mid September, Sun, Mon, Tues, Thurs 10.30-5
Party Rates.
Café.

Brantwood
Lake Road, Coniston
Tel: Coniston 396
Open: Easter-October, daily (except Saturdays) 11-5.30
Parties by arrangement only.

Brougham Castle (Dept of Environment)
Tel: Penrith 62488
Open: Mar, April & Oct: weekdays 9.30-5.30, Sun 2-5.30
   May-Sept: weekdays 9.30-7, Sun 2-7
   Nov-Feb: weekdays 9.30-4, Sun 2-4
Closed 24-6 Dec and New Years Day

Cartmel Priory Gatehouse (National Trust)
Cartmel, near Grange-over-Sands (380-787)
Tel: Cartmel 217
Open: Mar-Christmas, every day at all reasonable hours
Craft centre and shop.

Castle Dairy
Wildman Street, Kendal
Tel: Kendal 21170
Open: Easter-Sept, Wed 2-4

Conishead Priory
Priory Road, Ulverston
Tel: Ulverston 54019
Open: April-Oct, Sat & Sun 2-5. Weekdays by appointment.

Dacre Castle
3 m south-west of Penrith, near northern end of Ullswater.
Tel: Pooley Bridge 375
Open: only by written appointment and only in summer months.

Dalemain House
Pooley
Tel: Pooley Bridge 450
Open: April-Sept daily (except Fri), 2-5.15
Gift shop, tea room, picnic areas, deer park.

Dalton Castle (National Trust)
Dalton in Furness
Open: daily at reasonable hours, key from 18 Market Place

Dove Cottage and Wordsworth Museum
Town End, Grasmere
Tel: Grasmere 418/464
Open: Easter-Sept: daily (except Sun) 9.30-1, 2-5.30; Mar and Oct 10-1: 2-4.30; Nov-Dec by appointment only
Last admission ½ hour before closing.

Egremont Castle
South of the town.
Open: free access to the castle ruins.

Furness Abbey (Dept of Environment)
Barrow-in-Furness
Tel: Barrow-in-Furness 23420
Open: Mar, Apr, Oct: 9.30-5.30, Sun:
2-5.30
   May-Sept: 9.30-7, Sun 2-7
   Nov-Feb: 9.30-4, Sun 2-4
   Closed, Dec 24-6 and New Year's Day
Car park, picnic site, toilets.

Graythwaite Hall Gardens
Lakeside, Ulverston
Tel: Newby Bridge 333
Open: Grounds only, Apr-June daily
10-6.

Hill Top (National Trust)
Near Sawrey, Ambleside
Tel: Hawkshead 334
Open: Apr-Oct daily (except Fri) 10-
5.30, Sun 2-5.30, or dusk if earlier.
No reductions for parties. Refreshments
at Tower Bank Arms (also National
Trust). Number of visitors may be
restricted at peak times and considerable
delays may occur.

Hawkshead Courthouse (National Trust)
Hawkshead, Ambleside
Tel: Ambleside 3003 or Kendal 22464
Open: Easter, then May-Oct, daily
(except Mon) 2-5.
No reduction for parties.

Holehird Gardens and Lakeland Horticultural Society Gardens
Troutbeck, Windermere
Open: At all reasonable times.

Holker Hall
Cark-in-Cartmel, Grange-over-Sands
Tel: Flookburgh 328
Open: Easter Sun-Sept, daily (except
some Saturdays) 11-6. Last visitors to
Hall 5.15.
Party rates.
Gift shop, cafe, motor museum, adventure playground, children's farm.

Kendal Castle
Open: free access.

Leighton Hall
Yealand, near Carnforth
Tel: Carnforth 2729
Open: May-Sept, Wed, Thurs, Sun and
Bank Holidays 2-5; Grounds only Tues
and Fri 2-5. Open at other times for
booked parties of more than 26 people.
Parties by arrangement (reduced rates).
Cafeteria, gift shop, woodland walk.

Hutton-in-the-Forest, Penrith
Tel: Skelton 207
Open: May-Sept, Thurs 2-5. Also Bank
Holiday Mondays and some Mondays in
Aug and Sept.
Parties by arrangement Wednesdays end
of Apr-Sept.

Levens Hall
On A6 5m south of Kendal
Tel: Sedgwick 60321
Open: Easter-Sept: Tues, Wed, Thurs,
Sun and Bank Holiday Mon 2-5.
Gardens and plant centre daily 10-5 (not
weekends in winter).
Parties by arrangement (reduced rates).
No dogs. Licensed bar, cafeteria, gift
shop, steam museum.

Lingholm
Portinscale, Derwent Water
Tel: Keswick 72003
Open: Gardens only, daily (except Sun)
Apr-Oct, 10-5.
Reductions for parties of 30 or more. No
dogs.

Lorton Hall
Low Lorton, Cockermouth
Tel: Lorton 252
Open: By prior arrangement only.

Mirehouse, Keswick
Tel: Keswick 72287
Open: House: May-Oct, Wed & Sun
2-5.30
   Grounds: Mar-Oct, daily 9-6.
Open by appointment at most other
times; parties by arrangement.

Muncaster Castle
Ravenglass
Tel: Ravenglass 614; Garden centre:
Ravenglass 611
Open: Grounds and bird garden: daily
(except Fri) mid Apr-early Oct 12-5.
    Castle: Tues, Wed, Thurs, Sun 2-5
(last admission 4.30)
    Castle and grounds open Bank Holidays.
Parties by arrangement (reduced rates).
Garden centre, tea room, shop, nature
trail, bird gardens, teenagers' commando
course.

Old Windebrowe
Brundholme, Keswick
Tel: Keswick 72112
Open: Easter-Oct, Wed 2-4.30. By
appointment Mon-Fri 9-4.30.

Penrith Castle
Public park with free access.

Rusland Hall
Haverthwaite, Ulverston
Tel: Satterthwaite 276
Open: Apr-Sept, daily 11-5.30
Party reductions; no dogs.

Rydal Mount
Ambleside
Tel: Ambleside 3002
Open: Mar-Oct: daily 10-5.30; Nov-mid
Jan (except Wed): 10-12.30, 2-4.
Party reductions.

Shap Abbey (Dept of Environment)
Open: Mar, Apr and Oct: weekdays
9.30-5.30, Sun 2-5.30
    May-Sept: weekdays 9.30-7, Sun 2-7
Nov-Feb: weekdays 9.30-4, Sun 2-4
Closed 24-26 Dec, New Year's Day.

Sizergh Castle (National Trust)
Kendal
Tel: Sedgwick 60285
Open: Apr-Sept: Wed and Sun, also
every Thurs in July and Aug 2-5.45.
    Gardens: Apr-Oct: Wed, Thurs and
Sun 2-5.45. Closed Bank Holiday Mondays.
Parties by arrangement (special reduction). Shop.

Stagshaw Gardens
Ambleside
Tel: Ambleside 2109
Open: At all reasonable times.

Swarthmoor Hall
Ulverston
Tel: Ulverston 53204
Open: mid Mar-mid Oct: Mon, Tues,
Wed, Sat 10-12 and 2-5. Thurs and Sun
by appointment.

Townend (National Trust)
Troutbeck, Windermere
Tel: Ambleside 2628
Open: Apr-Oct: daily (except Sat and
Mon but open Bank Holiday Mon). Mar,
Wed only. 2-6 or dusk if earlier.
No reduction for parties. No access for
coaches. No electric light: difficult to see
contents on dull days.

White Craggs
Clappersgate, Ambleside
Tel: Ambleside 2376
Open: Gardens only, daily at all reasonable times.

Tytup Hall
Dalton-in-Furness
Tel: Dalton 62929
Open: all year round by appointment
only.

Wordsworth House (National Trust)
Main Street, Cockermouth
Tel: Cockermouth 824805
Open: Apr-Oct: daily (except Thurs
afternoon and Sun, but open Easter Sun),
10.30-12.30, 2-5.
Refreshments, shop.

MUSEUMS

This list excludes those buildings open to the public that have museums associated with them, or other places that have special displays, and are listed elsewhere.

Abbot Hall Art Gallery
Kendal
Tel: Kendal 22464
Open: Weekdays 10.30-5.30, Sat and Sun 2-5. Closed for 2 weeks at Christmas.

Abbot Hall Museum of Lakeland Life and Industry
Kendal
Tel: Kendal 22464
Open: Weekdays 10.30-12.30, 2-5; Sat and Sun 2-5.

Fitz Park Museum and Art Gallery
Station Road, Keswick
Tel: Keswick 73263
Open: Apr-Oct: Mon-Sat 10-12, 2-5; open until 7pm July and Aug.

Furness Museum
Ramsden Square, Barrow-in-Furness
Tel: Barrow 20600 and 20650
Open: Mon-Fri 9-5, Thurs and Sat 9-1. Parties by arrangement Thurs afternoon. Closed Bank Holidays.

Helena Thompson Museum
Park End Road, Workington
Tel: Workington 62598
Open: Tues-Sat 10-12, 2-4

Kendal Borough Museum
Station Road, Kendal
Tel: Kendal 21374
Open: Weekdays 10.30-12.30, 2-4; Sat 2-4. Closed Sun and Good Friday.

Maryport Maritime Museum
Senhouse Street, Maryport
Tel: Maryport 3738
Open: Easter-Sept: Mon-Sat 10-1, 2-5; Sun 2-5. Oct-Easter: Tues-Sat 10-12, 2-4.

Millom Folk Museum
St George's Road, Millom
Tel: Millom 2555
Open: Easter-Sept: daily 10-5, Sun 1-5.

Ruskin Museum
Yewdale Road, Coniston
Tel: Coniston 359
Open: Apr-Oct, daily 9.30-10 (or dusk)

Steamtown Railway Museum
Warton Road, Carnforth
Tel: Carnforth 4220
Open: Every day summer 9-5, winter 9-4.30. Locomotives in steam on Bank Holidays, and on most Sun from Easter to end of Sept, daily in July and Aug. Gift shop, cafe, picnic site, collectors' corner. Party rates.

Wetheriggs Pottery Industrial Museum
Clifton Dykes, Penrith
Tel: Penrith 2946
Museum, pottery, weaving and leather workshops, steam engine. Shop, play and picnic area. Caravan Club site. Tours for parties by arrangement.

Whitehaven Museum
Market Place, Whitehaven
Tel: Whitehaven 3111, ext 289
Open: Mon-Sat 10-5, closed Bank Holidays.

Windermere Steam Boat Museum
Rayrigg Road, Bowness-on-Windermere
Tel: Windermere 5565
Open: Easter-Oct: Mon-Sat 10-5.30; Sun 2-5.30 (other times by appointment). Special rates for booked parties. Work sheets, lectures, etc available for schools. Car/coach park, shop, refreshments.

VISITOR CENTRES

Brockhole National Park Centre
Windermere
Tel: Windermere 2231
Open: late Mar-early Nov: daily from 10
Films, lectures, exhibitions, nature walk, cafeteria.
Parties book well in advance.

Grizedale Wildlife and Visitor Centre
(Forestry Commission)
Hawkshead, Ambleside
Tel: Satterthwaite 272
Open: Easter-Oct: daily 9-5. Nov-Easter
by request.
Displays, shop, refreshments, 'Theatre in
the Forest', forest walks, picnic facilities.
Booking necessary for parties (tel: Kendal 22587).

Lake District National Park Dalehead Base
Seatoller, Keswick
Tel: Borrowdale 294
Open: end Mar-Oct: daily 10.30-1,
1.30-5.30. Groups all year by appointment.
A converted barn with interesting displays and study facilities.

Whinlatter Pass Visitor Centre (Forestry Commission)
Thorthwaite Forest
Tel: Braithwaite 469
Open: daily 10-5
Displays and nature trails, study room
and library for school use. Groups book
in advance. Picnic facilities.

COUNTRY PARKS

Bardsea, 2 m south of Ulverston.
Woodland and shingle foreshore, with a
nature trail and views across Morecambe
bay.

Fell Foot, near Staveley-in-Cartmel at the
southern tip of Windermere on the
eastern shore. Wood and grassland,
facilities for swimming, sailing, canoeing,
caravan site and holiday chalets. Administered by the National Trust.

Lowther Wildlife Country Park
Penrith
Tel: Hackthorpe 385 or 392
Open: Easter-Oct 10-5
Shop, licensed cafeteria, garden centre,
children's play area.
Party catering by arrangement.

MAJOR ARCHAEOLOGICAL SITES, excluding castles and abbeys

Carrock Fell Hill Fort, south of Caldbeck
village
A major pre-Roman hill fort, 800 ×
367 ft, whose walls must have been
massive.

Castlerigg Stone Circle, Keswick
A slightly oval circle (approx 98 × 108 ft)
with forty-eight stones remaining.

Galava Roman Fort (Borrans Fort),
Waterhead, Ambleside
Only the foundations remain of a fort
built about 100 AD which held about 500
men. Some of the archaeological finds
are at the Brockhole National Park
Centre, including the tombstone of a
Roman killed in action.

Gosforth Cross
An elaborate and slender Viking cross
standing 13 ft high, covered with carvings
showing a mixture of Christian and
Norse themes.

Hard Knott Roman Fort
One of the most exciting Roman forts in
Britain. Foundations of the stone buildings can be seen, including the headquarters, commander's house, granary
and bath house, also an extensive parade
ground.

Irton Cross, 3 m north of Ravenglass
A near perfect Anglican cross, probably
made in the late ninth century in Irton
churchyard on the far side of the church
among a mass of modern gravestones
(the cross in a corner is a modern copy). It
is carved with interlacing and intricate
knot work.

Langdale Stone Axe 'Factories'
Several sites have been identified amongst
outcropping basalt dykes, the best being
beneath Pike of Stickle.

Long Meg and Her Daughters, Little Salkeld, 4½ m north east of Penrith
A very large oval stone circle (360 × 298 ft) with twenty-seven of a probable sixty stones still standing. Long Meg is the tallest stone, 10 ft high, with symbolic 'cup and ring' carvings.

Mayburgh and King Arthur's Round Table
Near Eamont Bridge, 1 m south of Penrith
Mayburgh is a Late Neolithic henge monument. The circle is an unusual bank of water-worn cobbles about 15 ft high with a single standing stone, although there were others previously. King Arthur's Round Table is another henge about 60 ft diameter, although now damaged by roadworks.

Swinside Stone Circle, 1½ m west of Duddon Bridge, near Broughton
Although off the beaten track it is an impressive stone circle, with fifty-five stones, about 85 ft diameter. It is in a private field, but can be seen from a public path.

Walls Castle, Ravenglass
The bath house of the Roman fort Glannaventa, standing in woodland to the east of the fort. Although there is very little remaining of the fort the bath house walls stand 11 ft high.

Stone Circle & Avenue, Shap
A small circle of free-standing stones, partially destroyed by the railway line, south of Shap village is connected to an avenue of stones to the NW. The avenue ends with the 'Thunder Stone' in a field close to High Barn Farm.

High Street Roman Road
Only the route remains of this important Roman highway from Ambleside to Penrith.

STEAM RAILWAYS

Lakeside and Haverthwaite Railway
Haverthwaite Station, Newby Bridge, Ulverston
Tel: Newby Bridge 594
Regular steam services operated on Easter weekend and then daily May-Sept. Connects with Lake Windermere steamers.

Ravenglass and Eskdale Railway
Ravenglass Station
Tel: Ravenglass 226
Open: Late Mar-Oct, daily hourly service, limited service at other times.
Museum, cafe, shops, picnic area (at Dalegarth).

Steamtown Railway Museum
Carnforth
See list of museums for details.

MILLS
Some of these buildings have been adapted for other uses, but can be viewed from the exterior.

Ambleside Corn Mill
Near the town centre and although the site is now occupied by a shop the water-wheel has been reinstated. Ambleside also had fulling, bark, cotton and paper mills.

Heron Corn Mills
Beetham, Milnthorpe
Tel: Milnthorpe 3363
Open: Apr-Sept: daily (except Tues), 11-12.15, 2-5
Parties of more than 10 book in advance. Park in front of modern paper mills (Henry Cooke Ltd).

Little Salkeld Water Mill
Little Salkeld, Penrith
Tel: Langwathby 523
Open: Easter-Oct: Thurs to Sun 2-5.30; Nov-Christmas and Mar-Easter: weekdays only. Also open Wed afternoons in July and Aug.

Muncaster Mill
Ravenglass
Tel: Ravenglass 226
Open: daily (except Sat) 11-6.

Stock Ghyll Corn Mill
Ambleside
This four-storey mill can be seen on the far bank of the gill, and has been converted into holiday flats.

OTHER PLACES OF INTEREST TO VISIT

Calder Hall Nuclear Power Station
Windscale and Calder Works, Sellafield, Seascale
Tel: Seascale 333, ext 220
Open: Mon-Fri (excluding Bank Holidays) 10-1.30.
Visits by appointment 2 months in advance, minimum age 12 years.

Cumbria Crystal
Lightburn Road, Ulverston
Tel: Ulverston 54400
Open: Mon-Fri 8-4, also Jun-Sept: Sat 9-12. Closed Christmas week, but open Easter.
Parties of 30 or more by arrangement. Modern glassworks making wine glasses, decanters, animal figures, paperweights etc. Shop.

NATURE TRAILS

Nature trails in the Lake District are run by such authorities as the National Trust, Forestry Commission and North West Water Authority. Most of the trails have their own leaflets which are obtainable from Information Centres or the beginning of the trail.

Ambleside Area

Loughrigg Fell, $2\frac{1}{2}$ m fell walk
Starts from Bridge House, Ambleside, has superb views of Rydal and Windermere.

White Moss Common, $\frac{3}{4}$ m woodland walk
Starts at White Moss Common, 3 m north of Ambleside on A591. Views of Rydal and Grasmere, with bluebells in May.

Arnside Area

Arnside Knott, 2 m
From the mountain indicator at the end of Sauls Drive, Arnside. Views of Kent Estuary, Morecambe Bay, Pennines and Lakeland mountains. Not suitable for children under 5 years old.

Coniston Area

Brantwood, Coniston, $3\frac{1}{2}$ m in three sections
From Brantwood House, woodlands, pastures, deep gorge, waterfalls, iron bloomery.
Open: Easter-Oct: daily 11-5.30, closed Sat.

Grizedale Forest
Start from the Visitor and Wildlife Centre. The Silurian Way is a $9\frac{1}{2}$ m long forest trail over rough ground and steep gradients, while the Millwood Forest Trail is only 1 m following a beck through oak, fir and spruce woods.

Muncaster Castle, Ravenglass, 2 m
Through rhododendron walks with views of the Esk Valley, passing a heronry. From main gateway to the castle. Also a $1\frac{1}{2}$ m tree trail.
Open: Easter-early Oct: Sat-Thurs 12-5.
Stanley Ghyll, Eskdale, 2 m woodland walk
From Dalegarth Station on Ravenglass and Eskdale Railway, through a valley with woodland, mosses, ferns, a gorge and waterfalls.

Keswick Area

Dodd Wood, $1\frac{1}{2}$ m
On the east side of Bassenthwaite, starting from the car park, 3 m north of Keswick on the A591.

Friars Crag, Derwentwater
Nature walk suitable for the disabled, from the boat landings on the east shore.

Johnny Wood, Borrowdale, $2\frac{1}{2}$ or 2 m
woodland and open fell. Superb view from High Doat (1,050 ft). from car park in Seatoller.

Smithy Beck, Ennerdale, 2 or 3 m
Forest walk from Bowness Knott car park, along the edge of Ennerdale Water.

Thirlmere. Two woodland trails
The Swirls trail ($\frac{3}{4}$ m) starts near the car park on the east bank while the Launchy Ghyll trail (1 m) is on the west bank of the reservoir.

Windermere, $1\frac{1}{2}$ m
National Trust trail on the north west (Claife) shore.

Whinlatter Forest, Braithwaite, $1\frac{1}{2}$ m
From the Visitor Centre.

Wasdale Area

Nether Wasdale, $3\frac{1}{2}$ m lakeside walk with shorter alternative
Starts near the Youth Hostel. Along the lake shore and riverside, through plantations, past a tarn and areas of bog.

Nine Becks Walk, 9 m forest trail
From Bowness Knott on the north shore of Ennerdale Water.

Windermere Area

Belle Isle, Windermere, 2 m
From the house, path runs round Belle Island, fine views of Windermere.
Open: mid May-mid Sept: Mon, Tues, Thurs, Sun, 10.30-5.

Brockhole, Windermere, $\frac{1}{2}$ m
From Brockhole jetty along lake shore and through woodland, with panoramic views.
Open: mid Mar-mid Nov: daily from 10.

Hampsfell, 2 m
Walk through woodland and open fell with items of botanical and geological interest, fine views. From Windermere Road, Grange-over-Sands.

Serpentine Woods, 1 m
Woodland trails from Serpentine Road, Kendal.

TOWN TRAILS

These show the visitor the interesting historic buildings and other features in the Lakeland towns. Follow the leaflets available from the local Information Centres. Town trails are provided for: Ambleside, Barrow-in-Furness, Biggar Village, Bowness, Cockermouth, Dalton, Furness Abbey, Kendal, Keswick, Lindal-in-Furness, Maryport, Sedbergh, Vickerstown, Whitehaven.

GUIDED WALKS

These introduce visitors to walking in the countryside; there are frequent pauses and routes are ideal for photography. Stout shoes (or boots for all-day walks) and windproof clothing is necessary. There is no charge and booking is unnecessary. Details from Information Centres. There are guided walks at: Ambleside, Bowness, Buttermere, Coniston, Dalegarth (Eskdale), Glenridding, Grasmere, Hawkshead, Keswick, Langdale, Muncaster, Pooley bridge, Seatoller (Borrowdale), Windermere.

VIEWPOINTS AND SHORT WALKS

These are easy walks for a leisurely stroll and many are suitable for the handicapped. All are of easy access, usually with good car parking, and some are just simply viewpoints.

Windermere, north-west shore. North from Ferry House. Lake shore access and views.

Cockshot Point, Bowness on Windermere. Lake shore access and views.
Borrans Park, Ambleside. Lake shore access and views.
Esthwaite. Access land.
River Brathay, Ambleside. Level, tree-lined path along riverside.
Biskey House, Bowness-on-Windermere. Viewpoint, but steep access road.
Tarn Hows. Viewpoint.
Old Brown How, Coniston. Lake access.
Coniston Boating Centre. Lake access.
Fell Foot Country Park, Newby Bridge.
Friars Crag, Derwent Water.
Great Wood, Derwent Water. Short woodland strolls.
Nicol End to Lingholm, Derwent Water. Viewpoint.
Surprise View, Watendlath Road, Derwent Water. Viewpoint.
Castlerigg Stone Circle, Keswick. Excellent views.
Station Coppice, Thirlmere. Viewpoint and short walks overlooking lake.
Messengermire Wood, Bassenthwaite. Behind Castle Inn. Peaceful forest walk.
Pooley Bridge. Riverside walk.
Glencoyne, Ullswater. Lake shore access and good views.
Gowbarrow, Ullswater. Lake shore access and good views.
Howtown Pier. Access area and lake shore views.
Glenridding Pier. Access area and lake shore views.
Kirkstone. Viewpoints.

RIDING AND PONY TREKKING

Below are some registered establishments; most provide tuition for beginners and many welcome children, but some riding experience is desirable. Rides range from one hour to a full day, and advance booking is usually necessary. Check with the Cumbria Tourist Board leaflet 'Riding and Pony Trekking in Cumbria' for further details and addresses.

Robin Hood Riding and Trekking Centre, Bassenthwaite, Keswick.
Tel: Bassenthwaite Lake 296

Hill Farm, Bassenthwaite.
Tel: Bassenthwaite Lake 498

Spoon Hall, Coniston.
Tel: Coniston 391

Greenhills Stables, Crook, Kendal.
Tel: Staveley 821327

Woodbank Farm, Egremont.
Tel: Egremont 734

Low Cock How Farm, Kinniside, Ennerdale Bridge, Cleator Moor.
Tel: Lamplugh 354

Fleming Hall, Gosforth.
Tel: Seascale 455

Bigland Hall Riding Centre, Backbarrow, Haverthwaite.
Tel: Newby Bridge 728

Tarn Hows Hotel, Hawkshead, Ambleside.
Tel: Hawkshead 530

Side Farm Trekking Centre, Patterdale.
Tel: Glenridding 337

Sawrey Knotts Hotel, Far Sawrey
Tel: Windermere 2105

Lakeland Trekking Stables, Troutbeck Hotel, Troutbeck, Penrith.
Tel: Greystoke 243

Rooking House Farm, Troutbeck, Penrith.
Tel: Greystoke 561

Ellerslea Trekking Centre, Roe Head Lane, Pooley Bridge, Ullswater.
Tel: Pooley Bridge 405

Roe Head Trekking Centre, Ullswater, Pooley Bridge.
Tel: Pooley Bridge 459

Limefitt Park Pony Trekking Centre, Windermere.
Tel: Ambleside 2564

Craig Level Riding School, Lake Road, Windermere.
Tel: Windermere 3572

Wynlass Beck Stables, Windermere.
Tel: Windermere 3811

BOATING AND SAILING

These notes refer only to small pleasure craft capable of transportation or towing by a family car. As the lake shores are often privately owned, public launching sites must be used. Vessels propelled by internal combustion engines are prohibited on the following lakes and tarns: Bassenthwaite, Beacon Tarn, Blea Tarn, Blelham Tarn, Brotherswater, Buttermere, Crummock Water, Devoke Water, Elterwater, Esthwaite Water, Grasmere, High Dam Tarn, Little Langdale Tarn, Loughrigg Tarn, Loweswater, Overwater, Rydal Water, Tarn Hows, Wastwater, Yew Tree Tarn. There is a speed limit of 10 mph coming into force in 1983 on: Coniston Water, Derwent Water, Ullswater.

Bassenthwaite Lake
Owned by Lake District Special Planning Board. Launching with the permission of the appropriate landowner.

Brotherswater
No power boats.

Buttermere
Launching from a beach alongside B5289. Permission and fee at Gatesgarth Farm or Kirkstile Inn.

Coniston Boating Centre, Lake Road, Coniston (Tel: Coniston 366).
A range of rowing boats, sailing dinghies and self-drive boats or up to eight persons are available for hire. There is a car and dinghy park with no overhead obstructions for mast-up parking, and a good gravel beach for launching. Landing prohibited on some stretches of shore. Power boats must not exceed 10 mph.

There are also launching facilities on Coniston Water from the car park at the north end of the lake (no power boats), and at Beck Leven Foot on the eastern shore (no power boats).

Crummock Water
Craft may be launched from a number of sites alongside B5289. Permission and fee at Gatesgarth Farm or Kirkstile Inn.

Derwentwater
Visitors may use facilities of Derwentwater Boat Club, Portinscale, Keswick (Tel: Keswick 72912).
Facilities for launching at Keswick-on-Derwentwater Launch Co Ltd (Tel: 72263), Mar-Nov. No powered craft over 6 hp.
Launching at Nichol End Marine, Portinscale, Keswick (Tel: Keswick 72742 or 73082).
Small boats may be launched opposite Barrow House Lodge by Ashness Gate, 2 m south of Keswick (National Trust). Launching from car park at Kettlewell, ½ m north of Lodore, no powered craft.

Grasmere
Canoes and sailing boats, Easter-Oct. Contact Padmire, Pavement End, Grasmere (Tel: Grasmere 409). No powered boats.

Loweswater
Small boats may be launched from road on north-east shore. No power boats. Permission and fee at Gatesgarth Farm or Kirkstile Inn.

Talkin Tarn
Permission from Cumbria County Council, Estates and Valuation Department, The Castle, Carlisle (Tel: Carlisle 23456).

Ullswater
Launching north of steamer pier by the Willow Trees, or beach at Glenridding. No power boats. Sailing craft, canoes, rowing boats launched at Glencoyne Bay 1 m north of Glenridding on A592. No power boats.
All craft (including power boats, max size 20 ft) launched at Howtown on east side of lake 3 m south of Pooley Bridge. Ullswater Sailing School, Glenridding (Tel: Pooley Bridge 438), sailing tuition, dinghy hire, launching, parking, Apr-Sept.

Windermere

All powered boats must be registered. Further information from the Lake District Special Planning Board, Busher Walk, Kendal (Tel: Kendal 24555) or National Park Information Centre, Bowness Bay. Launching sites:

Glebe Road, Windermere: Windermere Aquatic Ltd (Tel: 2121), and Shepherds (Windermere) Ltd, (Tel: 4031).

Ferry Road (B5285), Bowness (Tel: 2753), Easter-Oct.

National Trust land on northern half of lake, fees payable to Millerground: Millerground Cottage

Ferry House to Wray Castle: Harrowslack Cottage, Far Sawrey

South of Waterhead Marine Filling Station: Merlewood, Borrans Road, Ambleside

Waterhead Marine Ltd (Tel: Ambleside 2424).

Waterhead, Ambleside, launch from beach, but access difficult.

Low Wood Hotel, 1 m south of Ambleside (Tel: Ambleside 3338).

Fell Foot Park, Newby Bridge, off A592 at southern end of lake (Tel: Newby Bridge 273). No power boats.

FISHING

The lakes and rivers of Cumbria provide good fishing for char, eels, perch, pike, brown trout, sea trout and salmon, but it is essential to obtain the necessary licence and permit (and the landowner's consent if you are fishing from the shore). The close season must be strictly observed. All waters come under the control of the North West Water Authority. Licences are obtained from the North West Water Authority, Rivers Division, New Town House, Buttermarket Street, Warrington, Cheshire or from local distributors throughout the area.

To fish in waters let to or owned by clubs, associations or other bodies you must buy a permit, often available from licence distributors. Information Centres have full details of permit requirements.

Rowing boats may be hired for fishing at Crummock Water, Grasmere, Buttermere, Derwent Water, Loweswater, Coniston Water, Esthwaite Water, Ullswater and Windermere. Some of these also hire out fishing tackle, and there are tackle shops in Bowness, Cockermouth, Kendal and Keswick.

CYCLING AND CYCLE HIRE

Cycling provides a pleasant alternative to fell walking or motoring, with numerous minor roads and lanes. The central region has some roads that are steep for cycling and will suit the energetic cyclist best, while more leisurely rides are to be found towards the coast. A number of recommended cycle routes are given in the Cumbria Tourist Board leaflet 'Cycling in Cumbria'. Cycles may be hired from:

Ghyll Side Cycle Shop,
Bridge Street, Ambleside
Tel: Ambleside 3592

Harpers Cycles,
1-2 Middlegate, Penrith
Tel: Penrith 64475

Keswick Cycle Hire,
Pack Horse Court, Keswick
Tel: Braithwaite 273

Lakeland Cycles,
104 Stricklandgate, Kendal
Tel: Kendal 23552

John Peel Garage,
Market Place, Cockermouth
Tel: Cockermouth 822113

Rent-a-Bike,
72 Craig Walk, Bowness
Tel: Windermere 2888

Rentacamp Leisure Hire,
Station Buildings, Windermere
Tel: Windermere 4786

Treetops Ltd,
Pooley Bridge
Tel: Pooley Bridge 267

SPORTS CENTRES

Whitehaven Sports Centre,.
Tel: Whitehaven 5666

Workington Sports Centre,
Moorclose, Tel: Workington 2105

SWIMMING POOLS

There are public swimming pools at the larger centres in and around the Lake District:

Barrow-in-Furness,	Tel: 20706
Egremont,	Tel: 820465
Grange-over-Sands	
(outdoor seawater pool)	Tel: 3053
Penrith,	Tel: 63450
Wigton,	Tel: 2412
Whitehaven,	Tel: 3113 and 5021
Workington,	Tel: 4258
Ulverston,	Tel: 54110
Windermere,	Tel: 3243
Kendal,	Tel: 20337

SPORTS AND LOCAL EVENTS

Grasmere Sports
The Lake District's most celebrated annual event, held on the third Thursday after the first Monday in August. Events include fell racing, hound trails, Cumberland and Westmorland wrestling, pole leaping, high leaping, long leaping and flat racing. Annual sports also take place at Ambleside.

Hound Trailing
The dogs follow a roughly circular course following a trail of paraffin and aniseed. the trail is 4½-5 miles long for puppies and 9-10 miles for dogs 2-9 years old. the events take place at various locations from April to October on Monday, Tuesday, Wednesday and Thursday evenings as well as Saturday afternoons and evenings. For details check with the weekly *Whitehaven News* published on Fridays.

Sheep Dog trials
These are held annually at a number of places, as well as at most of the agricultural shows in the region. The main events are at:

Applethwaite Common, near Windermere. First Thursday after the first Monday in August.
Rydal Hall, Ambleside. Second Thursday after the first Monday in August.
Threlkeld, near Keswick. Third Wednesday after first Monday in August.
Patterdale, southern end of Ullswater. Late Summer Bank Holiday Saturday.
Kentmere, Millrigg, near Staveley. Last Thursday in September.

Rushbearing Ceremonies
A traditional church ceremony with a procession of local children carrying bearings of rushes and flowers. It takes place at the following places:
Ambleside, first Saturday in July
Grasmere, Saturday nearest 5 August
Musgrave, first Saturday in July
Urswick, Sunday nearest 29 September
Warcop, on 29 June, except when it falls on a Sunday, when it takes place on the previous Saturday.

Agricultural Shows
See the Cumbria Tourist Board leaflets for the dates for the shows which are held at Cartmel, Cockermouth, Ennerdale, Eskdale, Hawkshead, Keswick, Loweswater, Penrith, Wasdale, Kendal.

BUS SERVICES

Cumberland Motor Services Ltd
Keswick Bus Station, Tithebarn Street, Keswick.
Tel: Keswick 72791/2

Ribble Bus Company
Bus Station, Kendal
Tel: Kendal 20932
Also booking offices in Ambleside, Carlisle, Grange-over-Sands, Penrith and Ulverston.

Mountain Goat
Victoria Road, Windermere
Tel: Windermere 5161

Coach tours

Browns
Market Place, Ambleside
Tel: Ambleside 2205

Robert Furness & Son
Royal Oak Garage, 31 Helvellyn Street, Keswick
Tel: Keswick 72386

LAKE CRUISES

Windermere Lake Steamers (Sealink)
Lakeside, Newby Bridge, Ulverston
Tel: Newby Bridge 539
Regular sailings between Bowness, Ambleside and Lakeside.

Ambleside Motor Launch Co
Waterhead, Ambleside
Cruises on Windermere, Easter to Nov.

Ullswater Lake Steamers
Ullswater Navigation and Transit Co Ltd
13 Maude Street, Kendal
Tel: Kendal 21626 and Glenridding 229
Three main return sailings from Glenridding to Pooley Bridge at 11.30, 2 and 4.30, April-Oct.

Derwent Water Launches
29 Manor Park, Keswick
Tel: Keswick 72263 and Borrowdale 282
Cruises on Derwent Water, March to early Nov.

GOLF

There is a wide range of golf courses in Cumbria and most welcome visitors. Booking is sometimes necessary, particularly for parties. All are 18 holes unless otherwise stated.

Barrow Golf Club, Rakesmoor Lane, Hawcoat, Barrow-in-Furness. (Tel: Barrow 25444)

Cockermouth Golf Club, Embleton, Cockermouth. (Tel: Bassenthwaite Lake 223)

Dunnerholme Golf Club, Askham-in-Furness. (Tel: Dalton-in-Furness 62675) 10 holes

Furness Golf Club, Central Drive, Walney Island, Barrow-in-Furness. (Tel: Barrow 41232)

Grange Fell Golf Club, Fell Road, Grange-over-Sands. (Tel: Grange-over-Sands 2536) 9 holes

Grange-over-Sands Golf Club, Meathop Road, Grange-over-Sands. (Tel: 3180)

Kendal Golf Club, The Heights, Kendal. (Tel: Kendal 24079)

Maryport Golf Club, Back End, Maryport. (Tel: Maryport 2605) 11 holes

Penrith Golf Club, Salkeld Road, Penrith. (Tel: Penrith 62217)

Seascale Golf Club, The Banks, Seascale. (Tel: Seascale 202)

Sedbergh Golf Club, The Riggs, Millthrop, Sedbergh. (Tel: Sedbergh 20659) 9 holes

Silecroft Golf Club, Millom. 9 holes

Ulverston Golf Club, Bardsea Park, Ulverston. (Tel: Ulverston 52824)

Windermere Golf Club, Cleabarrow, Windermere (Tel: Windermere 3123)

Workington Golf Club, Branthwaite Road, Workington. (Tel: Workington 3460)

ACCOMMODATION

The Lake District provides a wide range of accommodation from luxury hotels to simple campsites. It is not possible to list them in this book, but detailed lists can be obtained from the Cumbria Tourist Board or Information Centres. Also a register of hotels, guest houses, self catering facilities, caravan and camping sites is available from South Lakeland District Council, Amenities, Recreation and Tourism Department, 'Ashleigh', Windermere (Tel: Windermere 2244). A guide to Keswick is produced by the Keswick Publicity Association, The Council Offices, Keswick (Tel: Keswick 72645) which contains a list of accommodation in the area. During the summer months an information centre is run by the Association from the Moot Hall, Keswick, where an up-to-date register of vacancies is kept.

The area is rich in craftsmen who work with a wide range of materials, usually in the traditional methods. In most of these the visitor can see the craftsmen at work, but this cannot always be guaranteed, so check beforehand. The products are usually available for sale, and commissions are often accepted for specially made items.

Balnakeil Forge, Lamplugh Corner, Cockermouth (Tel: Cockermouth 823169). Mon-Sat 8-5.30. Metalwork.

Craftsmen of Cumbria, Fallbarrow Road, Bowness (Tel: Windermere 2959). June-Aug daily 9.30-6; Thurs-Sun in Apr, May, Sept and Oct. Pottery, leatherwork, metalwork, brass rubbing, jewellery, clock restoring

Cumbria Crystal Ltd, Lightburn Road, Ulverston (Tel: Ulverston 54400). Mon-Fri 8-4, Sat 8-11. Glass blowing.

Wendy Todd Textiles, Corn Mill Galleries, Old Town Mill, Ulverston (Tel: Ulverston 54600). Tues-Sat 9.30-5.30. Screen printing.

Whitehaven Workshop, 48-9 Roper St, Whitehaven. Mon-Sat 10-5.30, except Wed 10-12. Pottery and Batik.

Robert Davies, Holly Gate, Levens, Kendal (Tel: Sedgwick 60482). Mon-Fri 9.30-4. Keyboard instruments.

Susan Foster, 9 Windermere Road, Kendal (Tel: Kendal 26494). Wed, Fri, Sat 10-5; July and Aug Mon-Sat. Weaving.

Peter Hall Woodcraft, Danes Road, Staveley, Kendal (Tel: Staveley 821-633). Mon-Fri 9-6, Sat 9-1. Traditional Furniture.

Kirkstone Galleries, Skelwith Bridge, Ambleside (Tel: Ambleside 3296). Workshop: Mon-Fri 8-5; shop and showroom 9-5.30. (Closed Easter Sun and Mon, and Christmas week). Green slate ware.

Lakeland Stonecraft Ltd, 13 High Hill, Keswick (Tel: 72994). Mon-Fri 9-6. Stonework.

Little Arrow Pottery, Coniston (Tel: Coniston 381). 10-5 daily, except Wed, summer months. Pottery.

Pennine Tweeds, Farfield Mill, Sedbergh (Tel: Sedbergh 20558). Mon-Fri 9.30-12 and 1.30-5; Sat 9-12. Weaving.

Chris Reekie and Sons Ltd, The Old Coach House, Stock Lane, Grasmere (Tel: Grasmere 221). Mon-Sat 9-6, Sun 10-12.30, 2.15-5.30. Weaving.

Skiddaw Pottery, Rear Lake Road, Keswick (Tel: Keswick 73392). Open normal business hours. Pottery.

Wetheriggs Country Pottery, Clifton Dykes, Penrith (Tel: Penrith 62946). Daily 10-5. Pottery, weaving and leatherwork.

White Bridge Forge, Grasmere (Tel: Grasmere 414). Mon-Fri 8-6, Sat 8-12. Blacksmith.

Wolf House Gallery, Gibraltar, Silverdale, Carnforth (Tel: Silverdale 701-405). Jan-Mar weekends 10.30-5.30; April, May, Sept-Dec: Tues-Fri 2-5.30, weekends 10.30-5.30; June-Aug: Tues-Sun 10.30-1 and 2-5.30. Pottery and woodwork.

LAKE DISTRICT NATIONAL PARK

Head Office, Kendal, Tel: Kendal 24555

National Park Centre, Brockhole, Windermere , Tel: Windermere 2231

Information Centres (these also provide an accommodation booking service):

Ambleside, The Old Courthouse, Tel: Ambleside 3084

Bowness Bay, The Glebe, Tel: Windermere 2895

Hawkshead, Tel: Hawkshead 525

Keswick Moot Hall, Tel: Keswick 72803

Seatoller Barn Dalehead Base, Borrowdale, Tel: Borrowdale 294 (also a study base and interpretive centre for use by schools and groups).

Mobile Centres open in the summer months only:

Coniston, Tel: Coniston 533

Watershead, Ambleside

Pooley Bridge, Tel: Pooley Bridge 530

Glenridding, Tel: Glenridding 414

Caravan advisory service, Tel: Windermere 5555

Weather advisory service, Tel: Windermere 5151 (updated at 8.15 and 4 pm daily).

TOURIST INFORMATION CENTRES

run by local authorities with the assistance of the Cumbria Tourist Board. Most run an accommodation booking service and some are open in the summer only.

Barrow-in-Furness, Civic Hall, Duke Street, Tel: Barrow-in-Furness 25795

Cockermouth, Riverside Car Park, Tel: Cockermouth 2634

Egremont, Lowes Court Gallery, 12-13 Main Street, Tel: Egremont 820693

Grange-over-Sands, Council Offices, Victoria Hall, Tel: Grange-over-Sands 2375

Grasmere, Broadgate Newsagency, Tel: Grasmere 245

Kendal, Town Hall, Tel: Kendal 23649, ext 53

Keswick (summer) Moot Hall, Market Square, Tel: Keswick 72803 (winter) Council Offices, Tel: Keswick 72645

Maryport, Maryport Maritime Museum, Shipping Brow, Tel: Maryport 3738

Millom, The Folk Museum, St George's Road, Tel: Millom 2555

Penrith, Robinson's School, Middlegate, Tel: Penrith 4671

Ravenglass, Ravenglass and Eskdale Railway Station, Tel: Ravenglass 278

Sedbergh, Toss Lane Car Park, Tel: Sedbergh 21025

Ulverston, The Centre, 17 Fountain Street, Tel: Ulverston 522299

Whitehaven, Whitehaven Museum, Market Place, Tel: Whitehaven 5678

Windermere, Victoria Street, Tel: Windermere 4561

USEFUL ADDRESSES

British Mountaineering Council,
Crawford House,
Precinct Centre,
Booth Street East,
Manchester M13 9RZ
Tel: 061 273 5835

British Tourist Authority,
Information Centre,
64 St James's Street,
London SW1
Tel: 01 499 9325

Calvert Trust Adventure Centre,
Little Crosthwaite,
Underskiddaw,
Keswick CA12 4QD
Tel: Keswick 72254

Camping Club of Great Britain and Ireland,
11 Lower Grosvenor Place,
London SW1W 0EY
Tel: 01 828 1012

Caravan Club,
East Grinstead House,
East Grinstead,
Sussex RH19 1UA
Tel: 0342 26944

Council for the Protection of Rural
England,
4 Hobart Place,
London SW1W 0HY
Tel: 01 235 9481

Cumbria Tourist Board,
Ellerthwaite,
Windermere LA23 2AQ
Tel: Windermere 4444

Cyclists Touring Club,
69 Meadrow,
Godalming,
Surrey GU7 3HS
Tel: Godalming 7217

Department of the Environment,
(Ancient Monuments Commission),
25 Savile Row,
London W1X 2BT
Tel: 01 734 6010

Friends of the Lake District,
Gowan Knott,
Kendal Road,
Staveley,
Kendal LA8 9LP
Tel: Staveley 821201

Holiday Fellowship,
142 Great North Way,
London NW4 1EG
Tel: 01 203 3381

Lake District National Park Information
Service,
Bank House,
High Street,
Windermere

Lake District Outdoors Pursuits Centre,
Fall Barrow Hall,
Windermere LA23 3DL
Tel: Windermere 4824

National Trust,
42 Queen Anne's Gate,
London SW1H 9AS
Tel: 01 222 9251

National Trust,
North West Regional Office,
Broadlands,
Borrans Road,
Ambleside LA22 0EJ
Tel: Ambleside 3003

Outward Bound Trust
14 Oxford Street,
London W1
Tel: 01 637 4951

Ramblers' Association,
1-5 Wandsworth Road,
London SW8 2LJ
Tel: 01 582 6878

YMCA National Centre,
Lakeside,
Ulverston LA1Z 8BD
Tel: Newby Bridge 758

Youth Hostels Association,
Trevelyan House,
St Albans,
Herts AL1 2DY
Tel: St Albans 55215

YHA Lake District Regional Office,
Elleray,
Windermere LA23 1AW
Tel: Windermere 2301/2

Index